HOW TO WRITE AND
SELL SHORT STORIES

Della Galton

Published by Accent Press Ltd – 2008
Reprinted November 2009

ISBN 9781906373337

Printed and bound in the UK

Cover Design by Red Dot Design

For Mum and Dad, particularly Mum, who still insists that I taught her to spell when I was twelve. I'm not so sure about that, Mum, but thanks anyway! My business side – if I've got one – definitely comes from you.

Acknowledgments

As always, I'd like to thank everyone at Accent Press for their support and encouragement. This book couldn't have been written without the help of many, many people, not least the ones who gave me quotes for it. (There is a full index of who's who at the end.) My special thanks go to Ian Burton, but I am eternally grateful to all the writers who contributed and who have by their kindness reaffirmed my long-held belief that writers truly are the loveliest people in the world.

Foreword

As an experienced and hugely popular writer of short stories, Della Galton is highly qualified to write this book for writers. Her ability to take readers out of their day-to-day lives and transport them into new and interesting scenarios has put her in the top league of short-story writers. Short-story writing should never be thought of as the ugly sister of 'real' writing. It is a skill, and is one of the most sought-after ways of getting your work into print.

It is a fallacy to think that there is only one type of short story, and that they must all be 'women's reads'. The women's fiction market is certainly the biggest one, but within that category there is a wealth of different stories to be told, from crime, to nostalgic, to humorous, to more traditional and romantic stories. Examining all of these in detail is only one aspect of this informative book. Short stories should entertain as well as appeal to readers, and Della pulls no punches in telling you how to go about it, and how to send your work to the right market to avoid the dreaded rejection slip.

Talent lies in the hands and imagination of the writer, but developing appealing characters and devising a plot that is not contrived is a technique that can be learned. Della shows how to write a story that will make editors reach for their chequebooks, which is what every aspiring writer wants. Short-story writing can be lucrative but also annoyingly frustrating when a writer is continually being told that his or her story is not quite right, and to try again.

Between these pages, you will discover some of the short-cuts to win over the most hard-hearted editor. These include the successful use of flashbacks, easy transitions, effective dialogue, and making the most of your characters' emotions. Above all, how to bring drama into a story without making it a melodrama. How too, do you convey changes of time and place within the confining length of a short story without making the whole thing seem too staccato? And how to deal with that ever-popular twist ending without giving the game away? These are all components of the short story which may come naturally to the experienced writer, but which are bewildering to the beginner.

Della's easy-to-read book not only tells you the way to do it, but shows you by example. Written with a light touch, but with the sureness of someone who knows exactly what she is talking about, aspiring writers will read this book avidly and learn a lot from someone who knows her craft well. More experienced writers will find it a useful dipping-in book to refer to when the elusive muse vanishes, or writer's block takes over. But since neither of those things appear in a dedicated writer's vocabulary, read, enjoy, and learn from it. This is a book that should be on every short-story writer's shelf.

Jean Saunders

Contents

Introduction

My journey as a writer began when I joined an evening class called Writing for Profit and Pleasure, run by a lady called Jean Dynes, way back in 1987. Or perhaps my journey began a little earlier than that if I think about it. My childhood was spent with my nose in a book – although if the truth be known this was because I was very shy and didn't make friends easily. Books provided a welcome escape. In books I could be anyone I wanted to be: a princess, a hero or a winged horse. In fact, anyone other than who I was – a gangly rather awkward child who didn't fit in.

It's amazing how many writers I've met who tell exactly the same story. Many of us read to escape and often we began to write for the same reason. Then we became hooked on the joy of writing and finally we wondered what it would be like to see our work in print. Maybe this is you, too.

As a child, I didn't dream about writing fiction. I was going to be a poet. My first ever published piece of work was a poem in Pony Magazine when I was eight. I suspect they published it because of my age, rather than for its literary merit!

My gran tells me I wrote her stories – and indeed has

kept a few embarrassing examples. But I didn't harbour any ambitions towards a literary career. Confidence was not my strong point. Although I was good at English – it was the only subject I was good at – I did not do well at school. I left with just two O-levels – don't let anyone tell you that you need a university education to be a successful writer. You do not.

There are other things you do need, though, and you'll need them by the bucket-load: determination; persistence; patience; courage; and the ability to exist on next to no money (or a second income) while you get started. Getting published is not a fast track route to fame and riches. But, saying that, seeing your first short story in print is the best feeling in the world.

Where was I? Ah yes, an evening class in 1987. I joined out of curiosity – and at the first class I attended, Jean Dynes asked if anyone had any success to report. A young woman stood up and announced she had just sold her twenty-seventh story that year.

I was impressed and amazed. And I knew in that moment that I wanted to be just like her. She was my first inspiration – her name was Tina Wade. All through my writing career, it's people who have inspired me. People who have helped and encouraged me, or simply people whose work I've deeply admired. Many of them were kind enough to give me quotes for this book. You'll find them under the 'tips from the experts' sections.

I hope this book will inspire you, too, but before you begin – a word of warning. Writing for publication is the most difficult, frustrating and heartbreaking pursuit in the world. It will leave you battered and bruised and despairing. It is also the most wonderful pursuit in the world. Nothing beats seeing your name in print for the first time. Nothing beats the feeling of complete strangers telling you they've been moved to tears, or enjoyed a quiet chuckle at the humour in something you've written.

The route to publication is a rollercoaster ride.

Enjoy the journey.

Chapter One

Marketing Short Stories

What is the secret of selling short stories?

Perhaps I shouldn't be answering this question right at the beginning of this book, but hey, life is short, and if you're anything like me then fitting writing in between the trials and tribulations of living is difficult enough, let alone having to read books about it too, so here it is:

It's really simple and it's also one of the things that so many would-be writers don't want to do. It lies in researching your market. This chapter concentrates on exactly how to do that and I hope by the time you finish reading it – that's if you don't want to skip it and get to the exciting bits about the actual writing – you'll agree with me.

So you really don't need to buy this book now, and you could of course stop reading and spend your money on something else. Or you might like to read on and learn some of the other tricks of the trade that I've learned during the last twenty years. The choice is yours.

Why do writers need a market?

Finding a market for your short stories before you've

even written them might seem an odd approach, but if you're serious about selling, then it is vital that you first study your market. Yes, that's before you even pick up a pen or sit down at your keyboard.

Here's why. Because writing is a creative pursuit, it's easy to forget that it's also a business. Your story is a product and if you are planning to sell it, then you must have a very good idea of who will want to read it, and therefore which editor is likely to want to buy it.

To put this in perspective, let's look at an example outside of writing. Let's suppose you are a door-to-door salesman and you are trying to sell the latest brand of miracle moisturiser cream guaranteed to knock ten years off a lady's age. You are unlikely to have much success if your first port of call is a youth club.

However good your miracle moisturiser is there is unlikely to be much demand for it from teenagers. If you are lucky, you might sell the odd one or two, but you are starting with the odds stacked against you because you have not studied your market. Exactly the same applies to selling fiction.

What are the markets?

Small presses
Small presses are a great way to get published when you are starting out – particularly if your style doesn't fit the requirements of women's magazines and you are not prepared to alter it.

The good news about writing for small presses is that they often ask for short stories that correspond to a theme, which can be very helpful.

The bad news is that they rarely pay much, if anything, for fiction – often a complimentary copy of the anthology or magazine your story is published in is the most on offer.

Details can be found in reference books such as *The Writer's Handbook, Writer's Market UK, Writers' and Artists' Yearbook* – and of course, the internet.

Short-story competitions
There are thousands of short-story competitions, some more reputable than others. They are advertised via writing magazines, fiction magazines, writing conferences, groups and classes, the internet and word of mouth.

Most charge an entry fee, which should correspond with the level of prize money on offer.

It is possible to win big prize money by entering short-story competitions, and I once had a student who was a very talented writer and regularly won top prizes, but competitions are a very hit and miss business because it's so tricky to work out what the judges are likely to choose. Unlike the magazine market it's impossible to effectively research the competition market.

Many short-story competitions also offer a critique service. However, do bear in mind this is only as valuable as the credentials of the person who's writing it. A critique written by a well known author currently working in your field is worth its weight in gold. A critique from a writer you have never heard of might not be as good! More on writing the competition short story in Chapter Seventeen.

Anthologies linked to competitions
The organisers of big annual competitions – such as The Bridport Prize – produce anthologies of prize-winning entries from previous years. These are a great way to study the types of stories that have won past

competitions.

Anthologies not linked to competitions
ome publishers produce anthologies of themed short stories. For example, Accent Press publishes anthologies of erotic short stories for women and invites submissions from writers for which they pay a fee. More on writing erotic short stories in Chapter Twenty.

The internet
There are hundreds of opportunities to get your short stories published on the internet – although in my experience there are still not quite as many opportunities to get paid for your work. This might change, but my current feelings about internet publishing are to proceed with caution. It is all too easy for your work to be copied or stolen.

Choose reputable sites when entering competitions or submitting your work for publication on websites or forums.

Radio
Writing for radio is an art form in itself – and if your chosen market is radio, then you will need to research your market in a similar way to which you'd research magazines. A useful website for writers interested in submitting radio short stories is:
www.bbc.co.uk/writersroom

Most of this chapter is about research and marketing and much of what I say about research for magazines applies to radio, although of course you will be studying the market from a slightly different angle – via the ear, rather than the eye.

Women's magazines
This is one of the most profitable markets in the UK.

No full-time writer can survive without them. If you are a man, do not be discouraged. Men write as successfully as women for women's magazines – more of that later. So, on to the business of selling your short story.

How to find a magazine market

Walk into any newsagent and you will see dozens of women's magazines on the shelf. Sadly the market has shrunk in recent years. Currently, only a small percentage of these carry fiction and some will only accept submissions from established writers or via agents. However, don't let that put you off. The magazines that do carry fiction are constantly looking for the perfect story for their readers. And you do not need to be an established writer to sell to them.

The markets for fiction are not static. I had intended to list the current magazines carrying fiction, but there is so much change in the industry that this information might well be out of date before this book is published. They are listed in *The Writer's Handbook* and *Writers' and Artists' Yearbook*. They're easy to spot; they are the magazines which have headings like 'Best Fiction' on their front pages. And if you're considering writing for them, you're probably already reading them. If you're not, you should be. So your first port of call should be to your local newsagent for a recce.

You may have friends who regularly read magazines carrying fiction, which saves you having to buy too many, but a word of warning here: don't waste time researching old copies. It's very important to read what's current. Even the stories you read in current issues will have been bought some time ago, but this is usually the closest you can get.

So, where do you start? The best advice I can give to the aspiring short-story writer is to start with a magazine you love reading. I'm strongly of the opinion that you will achieve success much more quickly if you write the kind of stories you love to read.

There's a reason for this – although it is possible to write by numbers and achieve success, you will do much better if you write from the heart. I believe that what comes straight from the heart goes straight to the heart. If you write honestly and with passion, you are likely to touch your reader. Write about what you care about. Do it with feeling – and there's a good chance your reader, including that first vital reader, a fiction editor, will care too.

What to do when you've identified your chosen market

Most magazines will provide fiction guidelines for would-be contributors. Write, phone or email your chosen market and ask for these guidelines. It's polite, when writing to enclose a stamped addressed envelope.

Fiction guidelines are an excellent place to start. They will tell you the technical side, for example, the length required.

Some guidelines will also state their preference for the following:

- First and third person stories.
- Male and female viewpoint.
- Multi viewpoint.
- Animal viewpoint.

They will also tell you what kind of stories their readers like, along with any taboo subjects or overused themes.

Some magazines like ghost stories and some don't. The same goes for crime, romance and twists, i.e. stories with a surprise ending.

Pay close attention to these guidelines and make sure you have the current ones. Magazine guidelines are often updated in line with their latest requirements.

When you begin to get published, many editors send out 'Regular Contributor' letters to update their writers on what they are looking for at that time. They are as anxious to get the right sort of stories for their readers as we are to write them.

Magazine editors will also tell you that while their guidelines give an outline of what they are looking for, there is NO substitute for reading their magazine. So once you are armed with guidelines, you will need to buy several current copies of your chosen magazine and study them carefully.

At this point, it is worth mentioning advertisers, which brings me back to the business side of selling. Advertisers have a pretty good idea of a magazine's target audience, hence the adverts a magazine carries can be very helpful to writers.

Does your chosen magazine carry adverts for stair lifts, face cream for older skin and personal alarms for the elderly? If it does, it is likely to be aimed at the more mature end of the market.

However, if the adverts are for vitamins for growing families, school uniform deals, or time-saving devices, your magazine is more likely to be aimed at a younger audience with families.

Pay close attention to adverts. It is also worth checking the letter page and the problem page if they have one. These are both good indicators of readership.

Who is your target reader?

By now, you should be getting an idea of who your target reader is. Let's say you have established that your target reader is a woman between 25 and 45, married with a young family.

If you can narrow this down a little more it is very helpful. There is no such thing as an average reader, but you can generalise a little – is she a full-time mum, or a career woman, or is she juggling work and family?

Once you have established who she is you can get a better idea of the kind of things she might like to read.

What kind of stories is he/she likely to be interested in?

Basically, she'll want to read stories that reflect her interests. The scope is endless. She is likely to be interested in family and relationship stories, she'll want to read about characters and situations she can identify with.

Back to men writing for women's magazines – as I mentioned earlier, women's magazines are by no means a closed market for men. But you will need to write about subjects that interest women. And you will probably – but not always – need at least one female character.

Your target reader will want to be entertained, moved, and possibly learn something new. Tread carefully with this last one – it's all too easy to end up writing a feature instead of a story.

It's also very easy to slip into "preach mode" particularly if you care passionately about your subject. Being too preachy is a common reason for a story to be rejected.

What is house style?

Every magazine has its own house style and it is worth studying your chosen market in detail. On the technical side, analyse the following:

- Length of sentences – are they short and snappy or longer and more descriptive?
- Percentage dialogue to narrative – does your magazine favour lots of dialogue or is there more emphasis on narrative?
- Is the magazine story told in first person? i.e. 'I knew the minute I woke up it was going to be a bad day.'
- Or third person? i.e. 'Sarah knew the minute she woke up it was going to be a bad day.'
- Magazines often favour one or the other. Some lean heavily towards a more narrative viewpoint, some will only take stories written from a single viewpoint.
- Past tense or present tense – some magazines won't consider stories written in present tense. If their guidelines don't specify, then check by reading several issues.
- Use of adverbs and adjectives – go through with a highlighter pen and see how many are used.
- All of the above make up house style – but although you can analyse until you're blue in the face – I'm a great one for analysing – the feel is important, too.
- Overall style – is the feel chatty and light and the writing conversational – or is the story more heavyweight and serious?

Check the tone of the fiction in your chosen magazine. Are the stories billed as heart warming, touching, poignant, or is the emphasis more on plot, i.e. tale with a twist?

If you can identify the feel of the magazine – you are halfway there.

When should you submit seasonal stories?

How important is it to submit stories for specific issues at a specific date?

Well, to be honest, most magazines will tell you that if they receive a brilliant Christmas story at any time of year, they will buy it. But it does help to submit them at the times when they are actively looking so they are not holding stock they don't immediately require. The following is a quick guide:

Most summer specials are compiled in January/February so write your summer stories early and submit them at the beginning of January.

Christmas specials are compiled in the summer, so you should be thinking tinsel, turkey and tidings of great joy around May for submission in June, at the latest.

A word of warning, although it's a good plan to write stories which are specific to dates in the year, for example, Shrove Tuesday, Fireworks Night, or any of the Saints Days, be very careful with less frequent anniversaries.

A writer friend of mine wrote a Leap Year story – she didn't sell it first time round, so had to update it for the next Leap Year. It's now sixteen years later and as far as I know she still hasn't sold that story!

I should have heeded this warning, but I have to confess I didn't. I still don't know what possessed me to write a millennium story, which I didn't sell, and is now redundant, as by the time the next millennium comes round, I shall not be here. There's a ghost writer joke there somewhere!

How to increase your chances of success

Now, let's assume you've done your research, identified the type of story your chosen market might like and written the best story you possibly can. Is there anything else you can do to increase your chances of success?

Well, there is one thing which is often overlooked. It's a numbers game – this might sound obvious, but if your chosen magazine only publishes one story a week, or even one story a month, then you have much less chance of breaking in than if they publish more than this. Some magazines such as *My Weekly* and *The People's Friend* carry several stories a week.

Many magazines also produce specials. Some of them produce monthly or bimonthly fiction specials. In addition there are the seasonal specials.

- Christmas specials
- Autumn specials
- Summer specials
- Holiday reading specials

Working purely on a numbers basis, you have far more chance of selling if you submit to a magazine that needs a larger supply of stories than one a week or month.

Word lengths

There is also the consideration of word lengths. Before you start writing, it is worth taking the time for a spot more research, which might help to tip the balance in your favour.

Let's say that you've decided to write a short story about relationships, of approximately 7000 words, because that is the length you feel would most comfortably hold your plot line and characters.

You've done your research. You know there is a market for this length, and this type of story and you are champing at the bit to write it. Should you begin?

Now, I'm not saying you shouldn't, but I would ask you to consider one last point before launching into your story. Exactly how many markets take 7000-word short stories? If your intended market rejects your work, can you rewrite and submit to another market? Or is this a one-chance-only opportunity?

Far be it for me to discourage a writer who is burning to write a longer short story, but in the interests of being published, I would ask you to consider this carefully.

If there are, say, ten markets for 1000-word short stories, and say, two markets for 7000-word short stories, it's not difficult to work out which of these markets offers the greatest chance of being published.

As I said at the beginning of this section, writing short stories is creative, but selling them is a business. Now, without further ado, let's get on to the exciting bit – the actual writing.

Chapter Two

Finding Ideas and Inspiration

Where to get ideas

Where do you get your ideas? This is the question I'm asked the most often and actually this is the easiest bit of writing. Before you throw your hands up in disgust and say, well it might be for you, but it isn't for me, just bear with me for a moment. First of all, what is an idea? My definition is that it's anything; an emotion, a situation, however slight, that could be made into a short story. It is the beginning, the spark, a fleeting snippet or thought – it is by no means fully formed. Ideas, as most writers will tell you, are everywhere in life.

Here are some examples of ideas that have struck me recently:

1) The extra hour when the clocks go back could be put to good use.
2) Chocolate is a substitute for love.
3) Why would a vampire be up a tree?
4) The bath is the only 'me time' many mothers have.
5) Makeovers don't just apply to people.

These are barely more than thoughts, but they all formed the basis of an idea for a short story, which was published. Later, I will illustrate how this process worked with one of them – from conception to completion.

An idea is anything that can be developed into a short story. It is usually something that interests you. But we writers are naturally curious creatures so it shouldn't be too difficult to find something that interests us. You might also like to consider the following as idea fodder:

1) An overheard line of dialogue.
2) An interesting news item – the quirkier the better.
3) An emotion you have felt – this one is very important for me because it can provide not just the idea but the inspiration needed to develop it.
4) A dream you or someone else had. These often carry direct messages from the subconscious.
5) Something that has made you laugh.
6) A person with a quirky characteristic.

The beauty of being a writer is that absolutely everything you hear, see, taste, feel, or touch can be turned into a story line. Your entire life is fertile ground for ideas. Each of us has our own unique life experience to draw from. As long as we're alive, we need never be short of ideas. Life itself is our story board, if you like. Writers often say, 'I can't write because I haven't got a very good imagination'. I'm going to say something controversial here. It is my belief that you don't need a good imagination to be a writer. All you need is the knowledge of how to develop bits of your life – or other people's – into a workable story line. It really is that simple.

I don't sit at my desk, racking my brains about what I can write next. I just draw from my own experience.

You can do the same. And in these chapters I will show you exactly how.

How to develop them

Developing a story line from an idea is simple. Ask yourself the following questions. Who? Where? What? When? How?

- Who – applies to the characters – who are they and whose story is it?
- Where – applies to the setting. Where does the story take place?
- What – applies to the problem. All stories must have some kind of conflict or problem.
- When – will the story begin or take place?
- How – applies to how you will tell the story. For example, will you use third or first person, past tense or present? What structure will you use?

Asking yourself these questions and thinking of the logical answers provides the plot of the story. Would you agree that so far we don't need much imagination, we just need to answer these questions? Hence, more logic than imagination is involved.

What's the difference between an idea and a plot?

A plot is the development of an idea – its logical progression if you like. The simplest plot is when a character is faced with a problem and then tries to resolve it. The problem part is important. If your character has no problem – then you probably don't have a story. We'll look more closely at this in Chapter Three.

Working straight from the subconscious

One of my favourite ways of working is to write straight from the subconscious.

This method doesn't require any imagination either. It actually requires you NOT to think. It's invaluable if you're short of time, and/or you don't have a clue what to write about next – both situations which I frequently find myself in! All you need to begin are a PC or a pen and paper, depending on your method of working, and some sort of timer.

Step one
Set your timer for six minutes.

Step two
Write as many first paragraphs as you can in the time allowed. These do not need to be long, two or three lines is enough. Writing first paragraphs is a skill which you will become adept at with very little practice. Try to ensure your first paragraphs have a hook, dialogue always works well, but do not think any further than this. Thinking about what comes next is inhibiting.

Step three
Set your timer again – this time for twenty minutes. Choose the opening paragraph that appeals to you the most and continue writing for twenty minutes. Do not worry about the resolution of the story. This is important.

Step four
Continue writing your chosen story. If you are not inspired to continue your chosen story, then either pick another first paragraph or go back to Step one.

Step five
If the ending of your story does happen to suggest itself

during Step three, then go on and finish it. If not, set the story aside and, more often than not, an ending will suggest itself when you're doing something unrelated – if not, then refer to Chapter Ten – what to do if your ending falls flat.

This method of writing consistently produces results. I think it works because the subconscious, when asked to provide ideas – particularly under pressure – will respond. It might take a little practice. But the effect is that you will stimulate your creativity. I've tried this exercise countless times with students and the results are amazing.

Another reason it works is because it requires you to launch yourself into writing without thinking. Like many activities, beginning is the hardest part.

This is one of those universal truths in life. Trust me, I'm a writer!

Using the same idea twice or more

As in journalism, you can use the same idea several times – copyright applies to the order of the words, not the idea. Let's take one of the ideas I mentioned earlier: makeovers don't just apply to people. Here are three of the storylines I've written and sold, using this idea as the kernel.

The analogy
The recently divorced main character decides to give her elderly house a makeover in order to sell it, but then realises that both people and houses don't necessarily need makeovers, they just need the right person to see their potential and fall for it.

The humorous twist
You think she is having a makeover, losing weight etc

but it is actually her golden retriever who's having a makeover.

The emotional twist
You think he is trading in his girlfriend for a newer, younger model, but it is actually his car.

These plotlines all stem from the same idea. But there are other ways to capitalise on your ideas. Change one of the following for a new and different story:

- The viewpoint of the main character.
- The setting.
- The age or sex of the characters.

How to inspire yourself

Set a story somewhere you love. The beach is always good for this as it's ever-changing and a wonderful mood setter. Or maybe pick a busy city you love. Or a town on market day. The latter two are great for characters too. I personally find houses very inspiring, particularly old ones.

- Choose an animal and attribute its characteristics to a person. Don't restrict yourself to dogs and cats – how about picking something more unusual? You'll be amazed where this can take you.
- Listen to a piece of your favourite music, and pick out a line or two of lyrics. Begin your story with that line.
- Dredge your memory for a time when you were inspired by a season, and then set a story there.
- Pick your favourite colour and use it as the theme of a piece of writing.
- Food is all around us – write a story set entirely around taste.

- Describe a character by focusing on one or two distinctive features. Give your character a problem and start writing.

Don't just read these suggestions, use one of them. Put down this book right now and start writing.

Tips from the experts

Margaret Mounsdon says:

'Never waste a journey. They can be a fertile breeding ground for ideas. If you're not fascinated by what is going on around you, and you can't get a story out of the gossiping couple opposite, then look out the window. What season is it? What's the weather doing? Is the train/car swaying, going fast, slow. Why? By now you should be teeming with ideas.'

Steve Beresford says:

'Ideas are peculiar things. I'm often asked by my fans (both of them, when they are allowed out of the clinic) where I get my ideas from. And I'll tell you what I tell them: I get most of my ideas from the One-Stop Plot Shop, which is a poky, dimly lit, old-fashioned kind of store next to the cake shop in town. It's run by a lovely old couple who charge £6 a sheet, or two for £10.

Occasionally, of course, the One-Stop Plot Shop is shut (Wednesdays and weekends) and then, if I've used up the professionally-produced stuff, I have to resort to coming up with ideas for myself.

Sometimes it can be really tough, but other times an idea can pop into my head, fully-formed, just waiting to be typed.

And ideas can be simply words or phrases or titles or bits of dialogue or snippets from magazines and newspapers or plots stolen wholesale from the television. These all go in a notebook that I can flick through to hopefully provide a spark when my mind is temporarily blank. But more often than not I'll use the One-Stop Plot Shop.'

Jane Wenham-Jones says:

'I feel a bit of a fraud giving advice on how to get ideas as I have the imagination of a pea! All I do is write down everything that ever happens to me. Writers can do a lot worse than to look to their traumas and some of my best short stories have been born from something going wrong.

I got a great story for *Woman's Weekly* when I reversed into an empty Ford Fiesta, smashing its headlights and necessitating several long phone-calls with its sexy-voiced owner (I never met him and he probably looked like a gnome but a Scottish accent always does it for me) and although I screamed the place down when my husband announced he'd discovered a rat in our garage it rapidly became a jolly tale of a mythical rodent and a birthday surprise. When my sister's cat got stuck up the chimney he found fame in Your Cat and when her bra wire got stuck in her washing machine it inspired a story about becoming a plumber. When I was writing for the magazines full-time, I became a dab hand at wringing a story out of anything. When the toaster caught fire or I lost my car keys, my first thought would be – once I'd finished stamping my feet and swearing – "what can I do with this?"

Of course if your life runs like clockwork and you never break down, leave your baby on the bus or forget to buy any food when you've ten guests coming to dinner you're going to have to write about what your friends do. Or do what I used to do when the muse deserted me and steal somebody else's plot (there's only supposed to be about seven in the whole world anyway). If you change enough details nobody will notice. Go to the dentist's (if you can find one) and go through their magazines. They're bound to be five years old and full of long-forgotten stories. Or get an ancient collection of tales from the library and give a classic a modern new twist. '

Chapter Three

Turning Your Original Idea Into a Workable Plot Line

What's a plot?

Plotting was one of the things that really confused me when I first started writing short stories. It can cause problems for the most experienced of writers. So what is a plot? Well, basically it's a series of events which follow on naturally without appearing contrived. But there is more to it than this. There must be problems and conflicts to overcome and there should be surprises along the way.

What's not a plot?

A plot is NOT just a linear sequence of events.

For example, boy meets girl – they get on well – boy ends up with girl. It's the oldest storyline in the world, but by itself it isn't a plot. It is merely a sequence of events.

In the simplest sense, then the following is a plot:

Boy meets girl – problem keeps them apart – boy ends up with girl, the problem having been resolved.

The problem can be anything you like. Consider the following list of potential problems.

- Their parents don't approve (Romeo and Juliet)
- Class is an issue (Titanic)
- One of them is married (Bridges of Madison County)

And some more, for which I failed to think of corresponding films:

- Race or religion is an issue – lots of mileage in these two problems
- One loves more than the other – or is more serious about the relationship, so you end up with unrequited love
- One is much older than the other

I could go on and on, but you get the picture. You can, of course, use a combination of these.

But that's not all there is to it. You also need to consider the structure of your story. Will you tell it using flashback – probably almost essential in a short story, i.e. how did they meet? What went wrong? More about structure in Chapter Nine.

You might also want to use some sort of device as a focus for the story. For example, in a recent story I sold to *Woman's Weekly*, called Love and Chocolate, I began with the statement: chocolate is a substitute for love. And then I set out to disprove this statement, which neatly rounded up the end and gave me my title.

Whatever you choose to do, make sure your characters fit the role you give them, and make sure your ending is satisfying, but not predictable.

Working it out in advance

Many writers know their entire story line before they begin to write, including the end. I very occasionally write like this, but on the whole I don't know what the resolution of my story will be. This is most inconvenient as I tend to go down many blind alleys and writing with no plot often takes longer. But it is how I work and how I am happiest, so I am stuck with it.

If you can plot out scenes, characters and storyline in advance and you are happy with this way of working, then it's probably best to continue with it. If you have trouble plotting in advance, or even if you'd like a change sometimes, then you might be interested in the next section of this chapter, which I call the 'plot as you go' method.

The 'plot as you go' method

Here's how I developed the idea of writing a story about the extra hour.

I decided that my main characters would be Claire and Andy. The story begins when they meet in Pembroke Woods. She is out walking and he is kicking his way through the autumn leaves, which she thinks is an odd pursuit for a twenty-something man. This is an extract from close to the beginning when Andy explains to Claire what he was doing:

"The clocks went back today," Andy explained. "So we get an extra hour. And I always try to do something fun with mine."

"With your extra hour?" I glanced at him curiously.

"Yes. Life's short enough, isn't it. I figure that if we get the odd bonus hour we should do something we enjoy." He hesitated. "That probably sounds mad."

"No, it doesn't. It sounds like the most sensible thing I've ever heard. I've never looked at it like that before. But now you've enlightened me, it's a tradition I shall definitely take up."

"So what will you do with yours?" he challenged, and we both laughed.

This is the point of the story. The theme – if you like – is that time is precious. It sets up something that will become a tradition for this couple: how they will use their extra hour each year to do something special.

Already, we are beginning to get a structure for this story, the readers now have the expectation of what Andy and Claire will do each year, which I will, of course, tell them. You see how the story is already writing itself?

Here is an extract from a little later on.

Over the years, the way we spent that extra hour became not just a tradition, but a source of great pleasure. Neither of us ever worried about the hour we lost in the spring when the clocks went forward, we just concentrated on the one we gained.

We didn't worry, either, about when the extra hour would start. It certainly wasn't at midnight – the official time for changing the clocks – it could be any time in the day.

One year we did a parachute jump. Another, we went rock climbing and once we booked a log cabin in the Highlands and spent the hour sipping mulled wine by an open fire and telling each other ghost stories while the wind howled eerily outside

One year, it coincided with me telling him I

was pregnant and we spent an hour talking about baby names.

Now, in order for this to be a story and not just a linear sequence of events, I needed some sort of problem. A problem and how it is resolved is at the heart of every good story. If there is no problem or conflict, then there is no story.

So, the next part of this plot development was simple too. I decided that the problem for this particular story would be to give Andy a fatal illness. Here is an extract from a little further on: (Nick and Louise are the couple's children).

Andy held on until the end of November. The week before he died, he told me he wanted one more kick through the autumn leaves before he went. Nick and I took him in the car to Pembroke Woods and then we pushed his wheelchair through the mud up to the woods. Louise held onto the side of it, as she'd once held onto the side of her buggy. She hadn't wanted to let go of babyhood, and now she didn't want to let go of her dad.

I knew how she felt. Nick helped me lift his father out of the chair and we helped him balance so he could get a good kick at those leaves. He was so enthusiastic about it I thought for a moment he might be releasing some of his own pent-up anger at long last, but when I looked at his face I saw only joy there.

"Cheers, I needed that," he said breathlessly, as we lowered him back into his chair. He was so thin at that stage I could have done it on my own, but I was glad Nick was there. I'd have

gone to pieces without him.

At Andy's funeral, I had them play Justin Hayward's Forever Autumn. What else? I don't think there was a dry eye in the congregation. Even the vicar had to blink and clear his throat before he launched into the age-old words of the service.

Notice the circular structure of this story – the couple met when Andy was kicking through the autumn leaves and they say goodbye just after he does the same thing. But this isn't quite the end of the story. Claire now has the problem of what she is going to do with her extra hour without Andy and how she will cope with the tradition they have built.

And now, a year later, I've survived Christmas without him. I've survived Valentine's Day, Father's Day and the children's birthdays. There is only one more anniversary to get through. The worst anniversary. The one where we would always spring out of bed and discuss what we were going to do with our extra hour.

Although she would like to ignore the anniversary of this day – her children won't let her. Nick says he has a surprise for her. This is the resolution of the story.

Then the side gate squeaks open and Nick appears. I don't know what I'm expecting, but it isn't for him to be weighed down by a tree. Its top end is swathed in plastic and Louise is carrying a spade and looking very pleased with herself.

"You can't plant a tree at this time of year, it won't survive," I gasp, as Nick plonks it in the centre of the lawn.

"Yeah, you can. It'll be fine." There are echoes of Andy's optimism in his voice and I bite my lip.

"Nick, it's a lovely thought, and I know what's behind it, but I don't think I can bear to look at an autumn leaf again – ever..." I break off and he touches my arm.

"You won't need to. It's evergreen."

I stare at him, not understanding.

"Then why? What's it about? Why a tree?"

"We thought – Louise and I – that you might like a physical reminder of Dad. Something to remind us he'll always be around. Here where it counts." He touches his chest and the gesture, so gentle, so poignant, causes my own heart to twist inside me.

"Forget autumn leaves, Claire. Think evergreen. No one you love ever truly dies. They're inside you. A part of you. We thought this tree could be a reminder that love always lives on. No matter what season it is."

"In here," Louise adds, and bangs her chest too, just in case I haven't quite got the point.

"Thanks," I murmur, not sure whether to laugh or cry, as I help them unwrap the tree and we decide where to put it.

An hour or so later, we wash the mud from our hands and I make tea and we stand beneath the white sky to drink it, breathing in the damp earthy smell of autumn, as we study our handiwork.

I'm not sure I will think about Andy when I look at it, but I'll certainly remember this day, when his children jolted me out of my self pity

32

enough to remind me that life really does go on.
That love doesn't wither and die, as they so
succinctly put it, but is eternal and evergreen.

Nick touches my arm, "Did we do good,
Claire?" he asks, sounding hesitant for the first
time.

And when I turn, Louise is looking at me
expectantly too.

"Oh yes, kids, you did good," I say, and I
reach out to stroke the leaves of the little green
tree, which doesn't look in the least put out to be
planted at such an odd time of year. And I know,
deep inside me, that tradition, as well as love,
will live on in this house – in all the years to
come.

The resolution also brings something else important
into the story – a universal truth, i.e. life, traditions and
indeed love all go on when you lose someone. At its
heart it is a story about healing and life after
bereavement. And all of this has evolved from the idea
I originally had which was – The extra hour when the
clocks go back could be put to good use. This story was
published in a *Take A Break Fiction Feast*, under the
title, The Leaves of Love.

Summary of the 'plot as you go' method

Give your character a dilemma to solve.

Preferably make it the sort of dilemma that will
force your character to re-evaluate his life or his
attitudes. In this way he will have changed before the
end of the story.

Be as nasty as you like. The tougher the problem
that your character has to face, the more drama you'll

be able to create.

Make sure the resolution to the dilemma is credible, but also make it as unexpected as you can. This is the tricky bit. Knowing you have to provide a resolution to the story before you start can be very off-putting for some writers (it is for me) so therefore I don't think too much about the resolution in advance. Unfortunately this can mean I get stuck sometimes.

What do to if your plot doesn't work

I once sold a story of 1000 words to *Woman's Weekly* called The Best Laid Plans, which I'd started the previous year and couldn't finish. Here is a summary of what I'd written so far:

The story opens with Katie in bed in hospital on her 25th wedding anniversary, which is not quite how she planned to spend it. Since she married Paul most of their anniversary plans have gone wrong. On bad days she thinks they're jinxed and on good days she thanks her lucky stars they ever got this far.

This was a light hearted story and the humour was provided by flashback (the story is in Katie's viewpoint) to previous disastrous anniversaries.

I got stuck at the 750 word point, which I frequently do. I couldn't think how to resolve this story. But because the story was already half written, there were only so many options.

1) They could have a late anniversary celebration which could go wrong.
2) As above, but it doesn't go wrong.
3) They could split up (not very satisfactory).
4) They could decide not to celebrate on the actual day itself, but at other times in the year, after all a

marriage isn't about just one day a year.

I stopped here because I'd found my solution. I used a mixture of number 2 and 4.

Plotting is actually just a chain of events that leads your character to a satisfactory resolution and that resolution will largely be determined by market.

Problems finishing
When you're stuck on a resolution – try asking yourself the following questions:

1) What this is it that I am actually trying to say?
2) What is story really about?

The Best Laid Plans was a humorous story, designed to entertain, but it did have a serious underlying message – a universal truth, if you like. A wedding anniversary is the day that couples celebrate on, but the other 364 days of their marriage were just as important. They could also laugh about the things that went wrong.

The answer is in what you've already written
The seeds you've sown early in the story will provide you with the ending. Look at what you've set up carefully and then explore every possible option. One of them will be the right one.

The title
Another quite useful thing I've learned is that the title should underline the theme, as in The Best Laid Plans – so if you are the type of writer who knows the title before they begin, then this can be very helpful.

How to stick to the point

It is sometimes hard to know what and what not to include. What's the difference between valuable characterisation and self-indulgent waffle? I sometimes have difficulty in knowing the answer to this one myself. This is particularly tricky when you have written a section you really like, for example, a beautiful turn of phrase or an original way of characterising someone.

It's very hard to stand back dispassionately from your work and decide what is relevant and what is not. It's even harder to let someone else make the decision. In creative writing classes I've taught, wars have broken out over this very subject.

With this in mind, I've discovered that looking at published fiction or in fact other mediums, particularly television, can be enormously helpful.

Here's how. Have you ever noticed that if anyone has a cough in a television programme, be it a soap or a full-length drama, then it's never an ordinary cough? It's a symptom of some deadly illness. In real life we all have coughs and colds. In fiction this simply doesn't happen. I believe that this is one of the essential differences between real life and fiction. When you're telling a story, then everything you say must have a purpose. Not just coughs, but every piece of information you give the reader should move the story forward. If it doesn't, then it's superfluous and should go.

Sounds a little over the top? Think about it. The easiest example to use is probably a twist-ending story. In a good twist every sentence you write will, in some way, be pointing the reader towards the end. The art is to make the signposts ambiguous enough so that more than one meaning can be read into them. The writer's job is to nudge the reader in the wrong direction, without deliberately misleading him or her.

The twist is then achieved by revealing the one piece of information, previously withheld, which makes the whole thing fall into place. An easy mistake to make when writing twist endings is to go off at a tangent, so that much of the story is irrelevant to the twist anyway.

Making sure that every word counts isn't – of course – restricted to twist endings. Below are some of the elements to check next time you're editing:

Characters
Are all the characters essential to the plot? For example, could your main character's best friend and sister be condensed into one person? Do you mention a character early in the story who never reappears? It is sometimes essential to mention other characters such as waiters, taxi drivers, parents, but if they are not essential to the plot, then don't give them a name.

Look upon them as plot devices, not characters and don't be tempted even to describe them unless this information is essential to the plot.

Description
Is the extensive description of your character's house vital? Possibly it is, if you are using it as a reflection of the character and it is tied up with plot line. Otherwise, cut it. Is the fact that your character's boyfriend has a big nose really relevant? Possibly, if she's considering giving him his marching orders because of it – and this probably won't make her very sympathetic! Otherwise it could probably be cut.

Information
Do we need to know that your character's mother gave birth to her at home? If your character is about to have her own child, then maybe it's relevant, but otherwise it

probably isn't.

This might all sound obvious, but it's amazing how much tighter fiction can be when you really do make sure that every word counts.

And in the very tight frame of a short story, then every word must count. If ever I'm tempted to ramble on, I remind myself that no one coughs for nothing!

Tips from the experts

Elizabeth Dale says:

'Plot is everything. No matter how brilliant are your descriptions of setting, character and emotions, plot is what will make your readers read on. To hook them with a problem at the very start, put difficulties in the way of its resolution and then solve everything in a wonderfully surprising way at the very end will leave them – and you -very satisfied. If you can add humour or sadness or any other emotion, even better!'

Chapter Four

Writing Effective Dialogue

What is the purpose of dialogue?

Dialogue has three main functions. It gives the reader information about your characters. It gives the reader information about your plot. And last, but not least, it gives life to your work. Imagine how flat a story would be with no dialogue. However, it should never be there just for the sake of it. When you write dialogue, check that it does these three things (not necessarily all at the same time). If it doesn't, then it's superfluous and should be cut.

Dialogue and characterisation

Dialogue is a reflection of real conversation, but it is not the same. When we speak to each other, we tend to say much more than we should let our characters say. Below is an example of real life dialogue between a customer and a lady who works in a garden centre.

"Good morning Gladys, how are you?"

"Hi – I'm fine thanks, dear. How are you? The weather isn't great is it? It hasn't stopped raining for days has it? Is it raining out there now?"

> *"Yes, it is. Not much, but it's definitely raining. It's cold too, for this time of year."*
>
> *"Mmm, yes I noticed it was nippy when I went out earlier. Now what can I help you with?"*
>
> *"Oh – I'd like some roses please. A mixture if you've got them. They're for Mum, not me, would you believe someone stole all her rose bushes last night."*
>
> *"Oh no – how terrible for you. Your poor mum must be so upset."*
>
> *"Yes, she is."*

Not very interesting is it! This is because it doesn't move the plot along and it doesn't characterise. This conversation, which is fine in real life, is pointless in fiction.

The next extract is how it could be changed to give a lot more information.

> *"Gladys, I'm so glad I caught you. You're not going to believe this, but someone pinched all Mum's roses last night."*
>
> *"Not those beautiful roses that your dad planted?"*
>
> *"Yes. Mum's devastated. They were the last things he planted before he died. And now there's just a great big empty space in front of the kitchen window."*

It has a lot more impact, doesn't it? Everything unnecessary is cut and we are left with just the information that we need. Note that we have dispensed with the two characters greeting each other. Greetings rarely add anything to fictional dialogue

How much should you use?

There is no set rule, but, generally speaking, aim for at least 30% dialogue to narrative in a short story.

If you are targeting a specific market, which of course you will be if you're wanting to sell your short story, then check the stories currently being published and see if the editor has a preference.

A quick approach is to use a highlighter pen to outline the percentage of dialogue to narrative.

When should you use dialect?

Dialect can be effective, but it can also be very irritating to wade through a lot of it. If you want to indicate that a reader is speaking in dialect, you could just use it now and then for that character, but don't use it for everything the character says. If in doubt don't use it at all. It's possible to show your characters have regional accents by dropping in the odd word.

For example, he's a beautiful baby, could be spoken by anyone in Britain.

He's a fine wee bairn, is likely to reflect a Scottish character.

A Scottish character can be defined by the odd use of, wee, och, aye, etc. Be careful with this. It can be overdone. Far better to echo the ebb and flow of the language, than to litter the text with colloquial terms.

Incidentally, one of the best ways I know of doing this is to listen to a film depicting the accent you want to portray. Just as we can absorb languages by going to their country of origin, so we can absorb the patterns of language by listening to them.

Different voices

In my opinion, the number one golden rule for writing dialogue for the contemporary short story is that we should hear the characters' voices and not the author's.

Specifically, this means both in content and in style. Your characters should not all sound the same. Why would they? They will have different backgrounds, different accents, different influences, they will be different ages, different sexes, have different interests. What they say and how they say it should reflect this. It follows that the more you know about your character the easier it is to know how they'll speak. Characterisation is closely linked to dialogue – more of this later.

Giving your characters different voices is one of the most difficult things to do when writing, unless you're lucky enough to be an audio writer – by this, I mean that you hear your characters speaking in your head.

Ideally, you should be able to read a line of dialogue in a short story and know who is saying it without the use of dialogue tags.

Tricks of the trade
As writers, there are many shortcuts which we can use to make our characters sound unique. Below are some of them.

Pet phrases
In real life we all have pet phrases and favourite words – make sure your characters have different phrases/words from each other.

You know what I mean?
Well, well.
Now, look here.

Terms of endearment
Likewise, give them different terms of endearment.

Love, darling, sweetheart, pet, babe, honey.

Malapropisms
Malapropisms (mix ups with words, for example, under the affluence of alcohol) can be used with great effect in humour, especially when they are double entendres – it can be overdone though, be careful.

Class and education
Your characters' class and education (and not yours!) should be reflected in their dialogue.

Good heavens, darling.
It ain't my fault, mate.

Use of language
Even very simple things can characterise, for example, do your characters say, yes, yeah, yep, yah or do they just nod. Likewise, do they say, thank you, thanks, ta, cheers. Mum, ma, mummy, mam, mama, mother, etc.

Style of speaking
Does your character talk in long sentences or short ones? Does your character actually finish his or her sentences? Do your characters favour certain words or a certain sentence structure? For example, do they tend to start or finish sentences with specific words? I once knew a lady who finished every sentence she said with the words, "Know what I mean?"

More about characterisation and dialogue
If your characters speak in a certain way readers will start to make judgments about them, so dialogue is one of the main ways to characterise.

Script writers are excellent at creating characterisation through dialogue. Particularly script writers who are writing for already developed characters, for example long-running soaps or series. Check them out next time you're watching television. Preferably switch the subtitles on. You'll be amazed.

As writers, we have another tool – introspection. Is there a difference between what our characters say and what they are thinking? Thought and dialogue go hand in hand in fiction and can be a great way of building tension or conflict.

Direct dialogue

Direct dialogue is the term given to dialogue where no speech tags, e.g. he said, she said, are used. For example, this is an extract from a story called Today's World, published in *Woman's Weekly* between a grandmother and teenage grandson:

> *"Are there problems at school, Daniel? Is someone bullying you?"*
> *Grunt.*
> *"Is it the work then? Is that bothering you?"*
> *Grunt.*
> *"I was at school myself once, you know. I do know what it's like."*
> *Grunt, followed by a snigger.*

We know who says what because of the question and answer format, and also, I hope, because of what is said. Teenagers tend to do a lot more grunting than grandmothers! It isn't necessary to tell the reader that Daniel is doing the grunting.

Indirect dialogue is the term given where speech tags (he said, she said) are used. But there is another definition of indirect dialogue. It can also be used to describe dialogue where the character says one thing, but means something else.

How to lay out dialogue

Each time new characters speak, they should have their own line, and dialogue is always indented when it starts on a new line. As are characters' actions.

In the following example, taken from one of my stories called Visiting Time, published in *The Weekly News*, two ladies of a similar age are talking.

Mavis perched on the edge of the uncomfortable chair and regarded her friend steadily. Pam looked tired, she thought, and a little bit miserable. No change there then. She put on her brightest smile. "So how are you today then, dear? How are you sleeping now? Any better?"

Pam frowned. "No, to be honest. You know I don't like to moan, but I can't seem to get a decent night's sleep at all. It's the traffic noise, you see. People are so inconsiderate driving around 'til gone midnight. Decent folk are tucked up in bed by then."

"Perhaps they're working late," Mavis suggested.

"Coming home from the pub, more like." Pam sniffed disapprovingly. "Demon drink's what killed my Alfie. I think they should be banned."

"What – pubs?"

"Yes, ban the lot of them, I say."

"Even that nice one by the river that Johnnie takes you to sometimes? I thought you said you liked their carvery."

"Hmm, well I suppose they could leave that one. And talking of Johnnie, I haven't seen him for at least a week. Selfish little so and so. You'd think he'd be able to spare the time to come and see his old mum, wouldn't you? I mean it's not as though I can go gallivanting after him."

"He's probably busy," Mavis said gently. *"Sarah only had the baby a fortnight ago."*

Notice how there is some direct dialogue in this extract too – once the characters are established, dialogue tags are only needed sporadically. Direct dialogue only fails if the reader has to count back to see who is speaking.

This can be avoided by making sure the voices are right – as in Today's World. Or by putting in the occasional dialogue tag to clarify.

Tips from the experts

Teresa Ashby says:
'I love writing dialogue. With dialogue you can move a story on, show aspects of people's characters and also describe the person they are speaking to. "I can't believe you're so upset. It was just a dog." Speaks volumes about the speaker and the person being spoken to. But to make dialogue sound real, it should be cut to the bone. I think it can flow better if it is broken up depending on the pace of your piece. "I can't believe you're so upset," he said. "It was just a dog." Personally I don't like using words like interjected, exclaimed, declared and so on when a simple said does just as well. There is a place for those words, but overuse can jar. And of course, the tip of reading your dialogue out loud is a good one. You will stumble over

wrong words or awkward phrases and be able to put things right.'

Sue Houghton says:

An older female work colleague once told me if a woman doesn't speak in the first minute of a meeting, she won't be taken seriously. I feel that applies to dialogue in a short story – particularly in women's magazine fiction. Have the main protagonist speak within the first paragraph – in the first sentence is even better. Get her heard!

Chapter Five

Creating Believable and Sympathetic Characters

How to create a sympathetic character

Characterisation is the means by which you make your fictional characters appear to be real people. It is probably the most important part of any piece of fiction. If the reader doesn't care about your character, he or she won't read on.

So how exactly do you achieve this?

Perhaps we need to start with real life. Who do we care about in real life? Our families, our friends, certainly, but how about complete strangers? What would make us care about them?

Is it individual qualities? How about cleverness, beauty, niceness? How do we feel about people who exhibit these qualities? We might admire them, but do we want to read about them, know about them? Will they make us care?

How interesting is it to read about a very clever, stunningly beautiful, extremely nice person? Not very interesting at all probably, or at least not unless she had some sort of problem and these qualities helped her to overcome it. Then it gets a little more interesting.

How about courage and unselfishness? Would we want to read about people who have these qualities? Are we interested in reading about someone who faced adversity with courage and won through? For example, do we want to know about the firefighters who risked their lives to go into the twin towers on September 11th to rescue the people trapped there?

Do we want to know about the boy who was bullied at school because of his stammer and then went on to become a pop star?

Do we want to know about ordinary heroism – the day or events that changed an ordinary person into a hero? Chances are that yes, we do. As a race we want to see people with courage succeed. We want the underdog to win. We especially want him to win if he is facing a problem that could affect any one of us. If he is facing it with great courage and dignity then he will soar in our estimation. This is the basis for every good versus evil story that was ever written, and is also often at the heart of a rags to riches story.

We like characters who are flawed. We like them because they appear more human. We like people who win through against amazing odds. We can identify with them and would like to feel we could be as brave in their place.

So, to create characters your reader will care about, you need to reflect real life. Don't make your characters too perfect. Give them flaws, make them human.

Give them a problem to solve. Make sure it is a problem that is not of their making. A problem that your readers will care about. What the problem is will depend on who your characters are – and who your characters are will depend on the market you are aiming for. Did you notice how I slipped that word market into the equation? Funny how often it crops up in this book!

If you can get your target readers to really care about your characters, to root for them, then you are three quarters of the way there. They will almost certainly want to read on.

Naming your characters

Does it matter what you call your characters is another question I'm often asked, and the answer is a resounding YES.

Here's a contender for the 'worst opening paragraph in the world' competition.

> *Dora had always liked David. She was rather fond of Donald too, but he wasn't as good looking as David. Dora's friend, Dorothy had a bit of a thing about Donald anyway so it wouldn't have been fair to have pursued Donald. She would definitely have to let David know how she felt about him, though, and soon, otherwise Dorothy might well get tired of her prevaricating and just go off with Donald anyway, leaving Dorothy and for that matter David feeling dismal.*

Confused? You should be. So am I and I wrote it! This is a rather silly example of why you should think about your characters' names. It will avoid a lot of confusion if you don't use the same initial for several names. Also try to have a mix of shorter and longer names. Jo and Katherine, for example, are less likely to be confused with each other than Jo and Jill, or even Jo and Mo, come to that.

However, names are a lot more important than just

distinguishing one character from another.

Names can suggest all of the following:

Age

This is ever-changing, as names come in and out of fashion, but bear in mind that names do tend to suggest their owner's age. For example, the names Dorothy and Bert will tend to suggest older characters than say, Emma and Ben. Grace and Jack are currently top favourites for babies' names – and it's very helpful to check what the most popular current names for babies are. There are websites galore for looking at the origin and meanings of both Christian names and surnames.

Class

Writers often use certain names to reveal class. For example Clarissa or Humphrey might be used for characters from well-heeled backgrounds, while Debbie or Bill might be used to indicate the opposite. On the other hand, Deborah or William are quite different from their shortened forms. This brings me on to nicknames which are very important.

There is a world of difference between Frances, Fran and Franny. As there is between Albert, Bert and Bertie. Charles and Charlie, Josephine and Josie. You can also indicate your character's relationships by how they address each other. A mother might call her daughter Elizabeth; her friends might call her, Liz, Lizzie or Beth.

Personality

And last but not least – names used in fiction can be used to indicate personality. Fern might be a romantic character. Mrs Posthelwaite-Jones could be posh. Nigel or Jeremy faintly silly. I've noticed that Della is often used to indicate stand-offish and slightly snobby (Hopefully I've shattered that illusion!)

How much physical description should you use?

It's not usually necessary to describe your characters at length in a short story (unless their appearance is critical to the plot). A line or two will suffice and these should be threaded through the narrative. The following is the opening of a story of mine called Accident Prone, published by *My Weekly*:

I'll never forget the first time I met Colin. Our eyes met across an empty room, but it wasn't love at first sight – more terror. Colin was clinging to a rafter for dear life, the ladder having presumably just slipped from beneath him. And I'd broken into the house by smashing a pane of glass in the front door.

We stared at each other in amazement. Colin's amazement was tinged with panic I couldn't help noticing, as I bolted across and replaced the ladder.

"Cheers," he gasped, climbing down and wiping his ashen face. "Good timing. Another minute and I'd have let go. And my ankle's not long recovered from the last time I broke it."

I should have picked up on that – how many twenty-something men break their ankles regularly? But at the time I was too flustered. "What are you doing here anyway?" I asked.

"Painting for James and Sheila Clarke." He gave me a sideways glance. He had eyes the colour of Bourneville and he was attractive now he was no longer panic-stricken. "I could ask

*you the same thing. Didn't you just break in? I
heard smashing glass."*

We know that Colin is an attractive twenty-something
man with eyes the colour of Bourneville and that
currently his face is ashen. We might also surmise that
he is fairly athletic; otherwise he is unlikely to be
clinging to a rafter. He is likely to be wearing overalls –
as he is painting the house. So a lot of physical
description can be implied by what a character is doing.
It's not necessary to spell it out.

Here's an example from another story of mine called
Climbing Mountains, published in *Take A Break*:

*Our leader, Anton, was about thirty. He was
fond of saying, 'Right, people,' and rubbing his
hands together. Anton had black hair, blue eyes
and muscular arms and legs. He reminded me of
Dave when he'd been younger. Before middle
age and complacency had set in. Before our
marriage, once as solid as mountains, had
begun to crumble.*

Here we get two for the price of one – Dave isn't
described, but we know he's an older version of Anton.

Using viewpoint effectively

Viewpoint is one of the first things we become aware of
when we start writing. It can cause a great deal of
confusion amongst writers, but in fiction all it means is
through whose eyes we see the story.

Single viewpoint

In a single viewpoint story we experience the story
through the eyes of a single character. There are two
types of single viewpoint: third person and first person.

Example of third person viewpoint

Maggie sat on the stone step at the back of the shop and watched the sunlight painting pale gold stripes across the patio. This had been her dream for so long. Why then was she so unhappy? She put her head in her hands and cried. It was ridiculous. She knew it was ridiculous – yet she couldn't seem to stop. The tears fell through her fingers onto her paint-spattered overall.

Example of first person viewpoint

I sat on the stone step at the back of the shop and watched the sunlight painting pale gold stripes across the patio. This had been my dream for so long. Why then was I so unhappy? I put my head in my hands and cried. It was ridiculous. I knew it was ridiculous – yet I couldn't seem to stop. The tears fell through my fingers onto my paint-spattered overall.

The first person viewpoint is more immediate than using the third person viewpoint. The reader effectively becomes the *I* character and can relate more easily to the action than when viewing it through someone else's eyes.

Dual Viewpoint

A dual viewpoint story is – strangely enough – one in which we experience the story through the eyes and inside the heads of two characters. Their viewpoints can be separated, i.e. we begin by seeing the story through Maggie's viewpoint and then we change to someone else's. Or we just dart around between them both. The latter is trickier because it's more likely to cause confusion.

I strongly recommend that you stick to using single viewpoint until you have a few successful short stories under your belt.

Multi Viewpoint

A multi viewpoint story is one in which we experience the story through the eyes and heads of several characters – it's also known as head hopping. This is not a technique used much in short fiction – the length restrictions of a short story don't tend to offer a big enough canvas so it can be too confusing.

No Viewpoint

It is however possible to do the opposite quite successfully and not use a viewpoint at all, i.e. we never know what any of the characters are thinking, we just see what they're doing and hear what they're saying.

Personally, I find not using a viewpoint generally unsatisfactory. It distances the reader from the character and the story. But that is my opinion and might not be yours!

However, there are rules about viewpoint which if you do choose to use it should be noted.

Viewpoint limitation

When we have taken the reader into a character's head, then we should make sure that what the reader sees and hears is limited to what that character sees and hears. For example, our character cannot know what a character in the same room is thinking, although he could, of course, guess.

Changes of viewpoint

It's also advisable to avoid changing viewpoint too frequently, or the reader might lose empathy with the main character, or worse be confused about whose viewpoint we're actually in.

Writing in narrative viewpoint
There are other more subtle things we can do as writers to enhance characterisation. For example, it's possible when writing narrative to reflect the viewpoint of our characters by careful use of language. For example, if you're writing in the viewpoint of a child it isn't just the dialogue that should be child-like, but the language of the story should also not veer too far away from the language a child might use. It's easy to fall into the trap of describing a setting, for example, using language that is way outside of a child's understanding.

Here's an extract from my story Jack and the Unicorn, published in *My Weekly*.

Hardly daring to breathe, Jack stroked the gleaming neck. The unicorn trembled a little, but didn't run away. Jack knew he could have slipped a rope around the creature's neck and it would have let him. And he was scared for it because trusting a human was bad. The unicorn could get into major trouble with all that trust inside him.

Here, I've tried to stay in keeping with Jack's view of the world throughout the story so that his viewpoint isn't compromised.

The difference between showing and telling

Showing and telling is a vital part of writing effective fiction – and it is another aspect of writing that causes a lot of confusion amongst writers. So what exactly is the difference between showing and telling?

The answer is in the question, as they say.

Telling the reader what is going on in your story means just that.

Liz was unhappy. This is an example of the writer telling the reader what Liz was feeling.

Showing the reader means providing a visual image of Liz's unhappiness so the reader can see it.

> *A tear rolled down Liz's cheek and she wiped it away with the back of her hand. Where did all the tears come from? She wondered, with the part of her mind that still functioned through the pain, if there might be an endless well of tears*

Showing tends to take a lot longer than telling. I liken it to teaching. When I teach a class of students, I can either tell them about a subject, i.e. lecturing, or I can get them more personally involved, for example, by having a workshop where they write for a brief time.

For me, it's the same with writing. You can either tell readers what is going on by listing facts, for example:

> *Tony can no longer walk unaided because of a riding accident he had when he was a show jumper, but miraculously it hasn't put him off horses. It's his first time back at a show to watch someone else ride, and peoples' reactions to his disability are beginning to worry him.*

Or you can show them, for example:

> *Tony wheeled his chair across the bumpy grass. The air smelt of horses and summer and he felt energised despite the awkwardness of the transport – although he had to admit it was a pain not being able to get about as fast as he*

used to. One or two people looked at him askance and some flicked him embarrassed smiles before hurrying away.

"Excuse me," he called to a passing steward. Can you please point me in the direction of ring 2?"

The man turned and his face broke into a smile. "Well, if it isn't Tony Connor – how are you, mate? Haven't seen you around for a long while – is that thing a permanent fixture?"

Tony nodded, relieved at last to have found a friend.

So instead of telling your readers a barrage of facts, which they may or may not absorb – show them a scene and let them make what they will of it.

Being visual is important, but it's not just about being visual. Here's another example. This is the opening paragraph of You Won't Be Alone, a story of mine published by *My Weekly*.

It wasn't cold enough to warrant using up her precious heating allowance, but Alice had put the fire on for Sebastian. He'd been shivery all day, restless too, but now he lay on the rug, paws outstretched, looking relaxed. The rug had always been his favourite place, right from the moment she'd first brought him home as a gangly pup, with paws too big for his body and ears that bent over instead of standing up straight. He'd flopped himself down, blinked chocolate eyes and captured her heart, totally.

There is some telling in this passage – but hopefully a lot more showing.

We can ascertain without being told directly that Alice is a pensioner (she has a heating allowance), that something is quite seriously wrong with Sebastian who is also no longer in the first flush of youth. Alice probably lives alone. Alice loves Sebastian.

Here is a passage from later on in the same story.

Alice knew with an instinct borne of years that it would be soon. She didn't want to go to bed, come down in the morning to the still quietness of another one gone. She'd never been sentimental, all creatures must die, but there was a deep ache in her heart tonight.

Outside, the wind was getting up. She could hear the crash of breakers on the old sea wall beyond her garden. In the morning the beach would be littered with seaweed and sticks. In the morning she would be alone. She leaned stiffly against the arm of the chair, her hand still on Sebastian's head. She would stay with him until the end. It was part of the promise she'd made. Always to be with them. The clock on the mantelpiece ticked onwards and Alice, sleepy, but determined, lay with her dog, her face against the soft fur of his back, one thin arm around him.

I hope this passage conveys that Alice lives by the sea (the beach is important to the story). That we know Sebastian is going to die, and yes, she definitely lives alone. Also that Alice adores her dogs, she's had more than one, that time is passing, and indeed a visual image of Alice, shown by the detail, one thin arm around him. It should also be possible for the reader to ascertain that Alice is quite a tough old bird and will do what she feels is right by her dog no matter how it hurts her.

In other words, showing is not reporting facts. It's bringing them alive for the reader in an interesting way.

Don't report it – make it real. Make it come alive for the reader so we can see, hear taste touch and smell it.

Use specific details: Alice's thin arm around Sebastian.

Use the senses: soft fur, deep ache in her heart, crash of the breakers, leaned stiffly.

Use strong verbs: the crash of the breakers, the beach littered with seaweed and sticks.

(These last two are what I call snapshots – brief visual images the reader can hear and see – as in, Alice's thin arm around him.)

Dialogue

Now, on to dialogue. Dialogue is showing, but dialogue tags are not. Strictly speaking, the dialogue tag is the author telling us how the character spoke.

Example one

"There is probably a huge flood of chefs all wanting to compete for this honour," Pierre said in not very good English.

Example two

"Probably there is huge flood of chefs, all wanting to compete for this honour. Do not fret, mon amie, I expect they have the – how you say – backdog?"

Leave off the dialogue tag if possible and show us Pierre speaking in broken English. It's much more effective than telling us how he spoke.

Tips from the experts

Sue Moorcroft says:

'Characters should be allowed to act. This means they'll *react* and *interact*, as well. Different characters react differently to the same incident, to external conflicts or stimuli, to internal conflicts and to each other. Get your characters into conversation and the whole act, react and interact technique will happen automatically.

> *Jason could feel sweat gathering on his brow. 'Get out of my house!'*
>
> *With a cat-like smile Melissa sauntered closer. 'What's the matter, darling? Don't you think your wife will be glad to see me? Are **you** glad to see me? You usually are...'*
>
> *A gasp alerted Jason. Slowly, slowly, he turned to look at Ann framed by the French doors, pain in her eyes. 'Just what is going on?' she whispered.*

Just by sweating, Jason is reacting to a situation. It may be that he's simply too hot but, more likely, it's that the appearance of Melissa has made him anxious.

Melissa reacts to his anxiety (and, probably, to incidents earlier in the story) by being ultra-cool and enjoying his discomfiture.

Jason reacts to the sound of Ann's voice by turning to look at her. Because he does this slowly we realise that he's reluctant to face her.

Ann reacts to the whole scene with dread and freezes. Her voice deserts her, her eyes reflect her emotion. The character interaction allows the characters to act out the story with a combination of dialogue, action and emotion. The page is your stage and your characters are the actors.'

Francine Lee says:

'When I first started writing my characters were a bit static. I had lots of scenes where they were at either the kitchen table or on the sofa drinking tea/coffee/wine and talking. To get around this I wrote a list of all the things people do when they are at home. Washing, ironing, cooking, cleaning the fridge etc. It makes things easier for me to have this as reference and you can also reveal the character more through setting and action, how they behave, the manner in which they do things.'

Rosie Edser says:

'Once I have the basic plot, I like to visualise my character's physical appearance, clothes, mannerisms etc. From this image, it's then easier to step inside her persona, feeling the emotional reactions to events she's experiencing.

'My characters 'live' in my house. I see them sitting on my sofa, cooking in my kitchen, but they look and feel totally different to me. If I'm lucky, the words the characters would speak come to mind. When I get lost in the characters, it seems as if they decide what happens next, not me!

'Needless to say, this doesn't happen every time I write, if only it did! When that living spark isn't there, I find it is sensible to sit on the plot until I have a better picture of the people. I read somewhere that characterisation is everything. And though I believe there should also be a strong message to the story, I think it is true that the readers must care very much what happens to the people. They have to form a bond with them, if this doesn't happen, there won't be enough motivation to turn the pages.'

Chapter Six

Settings

What's so important about settings?

When you only have a limited amount of words at your disposal, then you don't need to bother with a setting – true?

Definitely not true. A well drawn setting is just as vital to a short story as it is to a novel. While it's true that you haven't time for reams of description, you still need a strong setting – after all, your characters can't exist in a vacuum. The art of creating a good setting in a short story is to brush stroke it in. If this sounds like a book on art rather than writing then that's probably because I see writing as an art. Perhaps the difference between a novel and a short story is similar to the difference between a huge canvas and a miniature. Both are beautiful, both require a great deal of work, but one is in miniature.

I have an artist friend whose job is painting tins – the kind used to store tea or biscuits. Her work requires the same amount of skill as an artist with a full-size canvas at her disposal.

How do I get setting into a short story?

For me, this comes down to being very specific with your choice of words. Here's an extract from The Berlin Wall, by Marilyn Fountain, published in *Woman's Weekly Fiction Special*.

> *I'm stuck in here – in "the kitchen". Pot washing. Trying to hear the mystery voice competition on the radio over the hubble-bubble of eggs boiling for tomorrow's packed lunches... and the bronchitic roar of the extractor fan... and the drum roll of an eight-hundred spin cycle... and Jeremy Clarkson booming from the telly. It's small, steamy, hot and claustrophobic and I feel like Ruby, the scullery maid in Upstairs Downstairs. Except it's permanent Downstairs in this house, even when you're Upstairs. I hate this ruddy kitchen.*

What a fantastic description of the kitchen – which is central to this short story, by the way. Marilyn uses not just visual and audio to describe her character's kitchen, but the lesser used senses, scent (hubble-bubble of eggs boiling) tactile (steamy) and she also lets us know that her character feels trapped into being a permanent servant. How many mothers can relate to that, I wonder?

Here's another extract from Away for Christmas by Adam Millward, published in *Woman's Own Christmas Special*.

> *In the centre of the room is what I can only describe as a 'pod' – all curved glass, a completely sealed bubble enclosing an egg-shaped tub and glowing with green light. Mum is perched on a shelf-like seat inside, arms*

wrapped around herself. She looks like a rather forlorn extra-terrestrial that's crash landed in its strange craft.

I try and budge the doors, but they're jammed. Though it doesn't look as if they're controlled electronically.

'The Jeffersons said the doors played up sometimes. I forgot..." Mum says, just about audible through the glass.

This is a description of a high tech bath, in which the main character's mother is trapped. Even though I've never seen the bathroom, I could visualise it clearly.

And here's one more from Away From It All by Hilary Halliwell, published in *The People's Friend*.

It's lovely at Mudeford. Like stepping back in time. A thin strip of white sandy beach fringes the bluest of sea. And you get that lovely seaside aroma of fresh air and seaweed instead of burgers and beer like some places. There are stunning views out to the Needles and the Isle of Wight, and, it's nice and flat for a stroll – I mean Power Walk...

Settings must be relevant, particularly if you're going to spend a lot of words on them.

Use specific words
Don't say green if you can say emerald.

Engage all the senses
Don't forget the lesser used ones in fiction such as touch and taste.

Bring settings alive with snapshot visual images
I stared out of the window watching the clouds drift by below us, like handfuls of cotton wool

pulled from a giant's medicine cabinet.

(From my story Time out of Time, published in *My Weekly*)

Give settings depth with emotion
The pink house was bordered by a dry stone wall and inside the garden there were apple trees where children would play on endless summer days, shouting and laughing beneath the apple scented boughs. My children – the ones I would have when I was grown up and married and safe.

(From another story of mine The Pink House, published in *Woman's Weekly Fiction Special*)

Us*e light and shade – just as you would in a painting*
Neptune's terrace was a different place in September than it had been in July, Nick thought, glancing around. Chrome down-lighters cast pools of gold across the terracotta tiles and shadows slunk behind pots overflowing with greenery. There was more depth, more perspective. From an artist's point of view it was far more interesting.

(From my story A Jaguar and a Sea Nymph, published in *Woman Summer Special*)

How much is too much?

If the setting is not vital to the plot, then don't describe it in detail, but thread in lines to illustrate your points.

For example, it isn't necessary to describe a whole room. Pinpoint a few specific details and let your readers paint in the rest of the room in their imagination.

He had an office at the top of the house, which held a leather chair, a huge old walnut desk and a row of wooden filing cabinets.

(From my story Bridges and Butterflies, published in *Woman's Weekly*)

Tips from the experts

Hilary Halliwell says:

'I make mental or physical lists in a note book! I may visit the sea or the countryside and write down *absolutely everything* I see from a swan settling on the sea to a discarded tyre in an inlet on the estuary. I keep a book of visual and mental images and I find it helps me bring a story to life. It's amazing what you forget about what you see in a particular place. Look at the tiny details, one mention of a small insignificant thing can bring something alive in a story.'

Chapter Seven

Flashback and Time Span

What is a good time span for a short story?

A short story traditionally covers a shorter time span than a novel. Just as there isn't the room for a big cast of characters, there isn't the room for a long period of time. Many short stories span a week, an afternoon, or even a few moments. A short story is unlikely to cover years, although there are always exceptions to the rule.

What's flashback?

Flashback is when your character's mind skips back to the past – obviously you can't do this without a good reason – whatever your character is thinking about must have a bearing on her current situation. Flashback allows us as writers to insert relevant information which has happened before the story began.

Does that mean I'm restricted to describing the events of an afternoon?

Not necessarily! This is where flashback comes in – although your character may begin her story and end it on the same day – she can remember events from months or years ago. Just as we don't always stay in the present moment in real life – neither are your characters restricted to the present.

Is it OK to use flashback in short stories?

It's fine to use flashback. In fact it's sometimes difficult not to, particularly if you start your story at the point of conflict or change. You may then need to go back and show the reader – preferably scenically – what brought the characters to this point.

What are the pitfalls?

The main pitfall is that if you use large chunks of flashback your reader may lose the thread of the story. If your story begins with your character talking to someone, for example, and then continues with your character going into flashback – if you spend too long in flashback, we may well forget about the conversation at the beginning of the story.

To avoid this, it may be necessary to go in and out of flashback so the reader doesn't lose the thread of what is happening now. It's easier to look at an example. This is the opening of a story of mine published in *The People's Friend*.

Excuses, Excuses

"Mummy, there are stars in the bath."

"Are there, darling?" Rebecca smiled, without looking round from the washing up she was doing.

"There really are, Mummy. Come and see."

Rebecca dried her hands on a tea towel and looked at her daughter's excited face. "All right,

I'm coming."

When she got into the bathroom, Chloe was already standing by the bath, pointing. "See."

And Rebecca saw that she was right. There were stars in the bath. Tiny silver and gold ones of the type Chloe's teachers put on her schoolbooks sometimes.

She knelt beside her daughter. "Well, well," she murmured. "I wonder where they came from."

"Out of the sky of course. It was raining ever such a lot last night." Chloe glanced at her mother impatiently. "They must've been washed out of the sky and fallen in our bath because we left the window open."

"Yes, I suppose they must." Rebecca sighed, wishing fleetingly that she could see the world through five-year-old eyes. Or even through twenty-nine-year-old ones, she thought with a stab of pain, because if she were still twenty-nine then Andy would still be here, they'd never have had that row, and everything could be as it was.

She shook her head, trying to clear the image of his face. She couldn't turn the clock back any more than she could see things in the same way as Chloe did.

"Do you think they came out of the sky, Mummy?"

"Yes, I'm sure they did." Rebecca glanced at the basket of bath bombs on the edge of the bath. She'd used a purple one this morning and there had been tiny stars stuck to the outside. They must have been all the way through it, judging *by the number there were. She hadn't noticed them when she'd let out the bathwater.*

The line 'Rebecca glanced at the basket of bath bombs on the edge of the bath' signals to the reader that we are about to go into flashback, albeit briefly, to find out how the stars got there. But we are in fact mid-conversation in the present, so we swiftly go back to the present with another line of dialogue between Rebecca and her daughter.

"What time is Daddy coming to get me?"

"Ten o clock. That's in half an hour," *Rebecca said, standing up. "So I think it's time you got yourself ready."*

"I am ready." Chloe lost interest in the stars and skipped out of the bathroom.

Later in the story, Andy arrives to collect his daughter.

"Everything all right?" He stood on the doorstep looking uncomfortable, his dark eyes anxious as if he were trying desperately not to say the wrong thing.

His nervousness made her feel guilty, which in turn made her feel cross with him, because he was the one who should feel guilty.

"Yes, she's ready for you."

"Great. Thanks." He blinked a couple of times, pushed his glasses back on his nose in that way he had that made him look particularly vulnerable. Rebecca hardened her heart and remembered why they'd split up. How much he'd hurt her. If she let him back into her life how long would it be before he did it again?

This last line is the signal to the reader that we are

about to go back into flashback again. The next line is the beginning of the flashback.

"I've booked your favourite restaurant," he'd said on the morning of her thirtieth birthday. "I'm going to have to meet you there, I've a meeting in Portsmouth that day, but I've booked it for eight thirty, that'll be plenty of time."

"Are you sure?"

"Of course." He bent to kiss her. "I know my timekeeping's bad, Becky, but I wouldn't let you down on your big day. Trust me."

Notice how once we are in flashback there is no need to keep using the pluperfect tense. After the line, *"I've booked your favourite restaurant," he'd said on the morning of her thirtieth birthday,* we continue the scene in flashback as if it were in the present, i.e. *He bent to kiss her*, not *He'd bent to kiss her.*

Using the pluperfect tense more than necessary would slow down the flow of the story.

So, in a nutshell, signal to the reader when you're about to go into flashback – and also when you're about to come back again. Keep flashbacks brief, and keep them relevant and you should avoid confusing the reader.

Tips from the experts

Adam Millward says:

'For me, flashbacks are a really helpful tool for getting across integral background information to the reader in an engaging way. However, they should come with two warnings; firstly, a flashback should not distract the reader from the current-time plot and, secondly, the flashback must not confuse the reader with regard to where it begins and ends. The best tip I've learnt from other writers to avoid confusion is to 'signal' the parameters, by using the pluperfect tense (e.g. The last time he'd thought of her, he had been boarding a plane...) at the entry and exit of the flashback. It's also a good idea, particularly in longer flashbacks, to make one or two brief references to the 'present', perhaps using one of the senses, to act as temporal anchor-points for the reader.'

Chapter Eight

Using a Theme

What is a theme?

In writing terms, for me a theme is something that can often, but not always, be boiled down to one word. For example, all of the following are themes:

- Revenge
- Loss
- Love
- Loneliness
- Atonement
- Class
- Theft
- Come-uppance
- Age
- Vanity
- Recovery

A theme can also be boiled down to a phrase. Here are some examples:

- The proof of the pudding
- Youth is wasted on the young
- What goes around comes around

The last one is the basis of a thousand plots, where the baddie gets his come-uppance at the end of the story.

Is it necessary?

While you don't have to use a theme, I think they are a useful tool for writers because they help you to focus on what you are writing. You don't have to know your theme before you start. Sometimes it will emerge as you write.

Themes are a great help when it comes to the editing process too. You might find you want to cut anything that is not directly pertinent to your theme.

How does it differ from a universal truth?

For me a universal truth is slightly different. My interpretation of a universal truth, which is also at the heart of a story, is something that is universally accepted, so that when readers reach the end of your story they will think, 'ah yes, very true.'

It's really reader identification – so you need to know your market well enough to ascertain what universal truths will work.

Here's an example of a universal truth in action, taken from a story called, Good Enough, by Janice Day, published in *Woman's Weekly Fiction Special*.

> *You can't grab at a baby's head and hold it firmly. It's a sort of metaphor for bringing up children. You have to cup your hand over the skull; shape your hand to it; feeling the life pulse beneath your palm. It's magical. And when you are gently holding your baby's head in the palm of your hand, feeling your child's heartbeat through its skull, you have no idea*

> *that it's always going to be the same, and that*
> *underneath the angry words and the worry and*
> *the despair, you're still after all just holding the*
> *baby's fragile little head very, very gently in the*
> *palm of your hand.*

This is a beautifully expressed universal truth that I think every parent in the world will be able to relate to at some level.

Overused themes

Of course, like plotlines, themes can be overused. So if you are using a common one, for example revenge, do make sure that your story is sufficiently different.

If you're aiming your short story at a magazine, they will often state overused themes in their guidelines. These change all the time, so do check what's current.

If you're writing for a competition where the theme has been set, then it is probably even more important to find a new slant on it. If the judges read the same story over and over again, they are not likely to be impressed by version number twenty-two, however good it is.

I find that a good exercise when you are given a theme is to jot down all the first ideas that spring to mind. For example, let's suppose you've been asked to write a story on the theme of death. What springs to mind?

I've made a list, although of course yours will be different. But here's mine: Funerals; wills; grief; family squabbles; old age; black clothes; wakes; cemeteries; churches.

The viewpoint character who springs to mind is a bereaved partner or child of the deceased.

Therefore, if I want my story to be different I'm going to have to discard these first ideas. Try thinking laterally by using the questions: What? Why? When? How? Where? and Who?

What?

What happens at your character's funeral? Does it have to be a sad event? This is fiction, we can go anywhere with this.

Why?

Why is the funeral taking place? Obviously someone has died, but was it a natural death or were there suspicious circumstances? Take this one step further – perhaps someone hasn't died, perhaps this is part of an elaborate hoax by someone faking his own death.

When?

Your story doesn't have to be contemporary. It can be set in the past or perhaps the future?

How?

Now on to mood – could you write a light-hearted story about a funeral? That would be a challenge.

Where?

Maybe you could write about a funeral set in another country where there are different cultures, different ways of saying goodbye.

Who?

It's not just old people who die. Does the deceased have to be old, or even human? Might a story about the funeral of an animal be different enough to catch the judge's or editor's attention? A story about an alien would be different too, wouldn't it? I'd love to read a good story about an alien's funeral.

While you're thinking about who – you also need to consider viewpoint.

Could your story be in the viewpoint of the funeral

director? Or a passer-by who is not directly involved, but who is affected?

Could the story be told from the viewpoint of the deceased? Or even from the viewpoint of someone already deceased, waiting to greet the newly deceased? Expand your horizons. Could the funeral be of the last person on earth?

Finding a new theme

'It's a familiar theme' is a common reason given for rejection by magazines.

I'm not sure if it's possible to find an entirely new theme, but as there are hundreds of themes it is definitely possible to find a less well worn one.

This comes back to research, once again.

Research your market carefully. If you are writing for magazines or radio, then compile a folder of several current stories and list the themes.

Then avoid them. Or use your own experience and try to find a new slant on an old theme. Or preferably do both.

Tips from the experts

Rachel Lovell says:

'The skill that evaded me the longest in my endeavours to get my first story published was that of creating a plot that worked. Short stories for women's magazines need to have a strong plot where everything gears towards a final dénouement. When I reach the end of a story now and see how the characters react to the conflict I've thrown at them I find I often discover a theme. I'll then go back over the story and edit out anything which is not focused on this. This helps to tighten the plot, I believe.'

Chapter Nine

Structure and Pace

Why should you use a structure?

All stories must have some kind of structure. Stories without structure are in danger of rambling, losing focus and generally becoming something other than a story. Rather like in a building, solid foundations are essential. Without them your creation might well collapse and you'll be left with nothing but a pile of rubble, or in fiction terms, a pile of words.

What kind of structures are there?

There are lots! I've listed a few, but you can no doubt think of others. Indeed, you might want to invent some new ones. It's good fun experimenting with structure.

The simplest structure is the one that people of my generation tended to be taught at school. Your story must have a beginning, middle and end.

I think this structure is still one of the best and some writers might argue that all stories must have a beginning, middle and end, whatever kind of structure you use. Perhaps they're right. You must make up your own mind. Here are some examples of different types of structure.

Circular

This is one of the classic short story structures. The story opens in the present – usually at a point of change, or when something exciting is happening.

Then flashback is used to convey events that have led up to this point. We return to the present and move forward a little for the resolution.

Here is an example of a circular structure in action. This is the opening paragraph of The Missing Aunt by Teresa Ashby, published in *Woman's Weekly Fiction Special*.

> *Lost.*
>
> *Miles from anywhere up a dusty track on a hot day with a leaky bottle of water and sore feet.*
>
> *Brilliant.*
>
> *Lucia sat down on a rock in the shade and tried to get her bearings. It was all that goat's fault. It was grinning at her now from the steep bank on the other side of the road.*

So we know that Lucia is lost – but we don't know how she came to be there. We will find out over the course of the story. If this story was starting at the true beginning, by the way, we would join Lucia and her partner Michael at the beginning of the walk. However, this probably wouldn't be too exciting because at that point they didn't have a problem. It's much more of a hook to join her when she has a problem.

Here are the closing paragraphs:

> *They walked to the other side and looked down the hill and there was their hotel, just five minutes walk away.*
>
> *"Thank goodness for that," Lucia said. "I*

don't think I could walk any further. I've so much to tell you, Michael."

And he'd so much to tell her. His idea for bringing Alice along next time for one thing.

Maybe they didn't have much in common, but they loved each and apparently they both talked to goats. You couldn't ask for better than that.

So, just to recap, we begin when Lucia is lost. We end when she has resolved this problem, not just the problem of being lost but her relationship dilemma. Another popular device for circular short stories is to somehow link the beginning to the end. In this case, it's achieved by the mention of goats. This helps to give a circular feel to the story.

Diary

As you'd expect this is when the story is told via diary extracts. They crop up regularly in magazines. I think the editors like them because they are a bit different.

Letters

This is when a story is told in the form of either one letter – or a series of letters between characters.

I once sold a story which was made up of a combination of letters and texts between mother and son (son was away at university).

Dates

This is when a story is broken up into headings: You could use headings such as:

- Hours of the day
- Days of the week
- Months of the year
- Seasons

Or indeed, you could use any significant dates you like.

Double handers

These are stories told using more than one viewpoint. They are split into sections, each section belonging to a different character. Often the characters' viewpoints are headed up with their names. You can use as many characters as you like, but more than three can be confusing in a short story.

More unusual structures

I once sold a story called Keys (2000 words) which was split into five sections. Each section skipped forward in time and began with the mention of a key.

I've also sold a story called Rain. Each section started with a mention of the rain.

You could apply this method using any theme or word. There are endless combinations.

The monologue

Although the monologue is not a structure, I thought this was a good place to mention them.

What is a monologue?

The word monologue comes from mono (single) and logos (tongue)

It is basically a speech by one person as opposed to dialogue which can take place between two or more persons.

As well as being a speech by one person, there is another aspect to writing a monologue. The speakers are usually giving away more about themselves than they realise. To illustrate this, here is an extract from one of my stories, which is written in a monologue style.

Confessions of a Cleaner, published in *The Weekly News*

You find out secrets when you're a cleaner, especially when you're cleaning folk's bedrooms. Not that everyone lets me in there, mind. Bernard, who I do on Wednesdays and Fridays when he's in the city, padlocks his bedroom door. At first I was a bit worried he might be locking someone in or something – you never know with these city types – so I went round the back and sneaked a look through the window.

There wasn't anyone in there, which was a relief, but there were mirrors on the ceiling. I knew there was something kinky about Bernard; I mean why do you need mirrors on the ceiling?

I'd love to have a proper look in that bedroom. I might have a go at picking the padlock one day. There's a website on the internet that tells you how to do it. (I came across it when I was looking for a knitting pattern.) Besides, Bernard's nets are filthy; I'd be doing him a favour.

Don't get me wrong. I don't go snooping through drawers. You don't need to, in my experience. People are very careless about what they leave under beds. You'd be amazed what comes out stuck to the end of my Hoover nozzle. I won't go into detail, except to say I didn't know those sorts of things existed outside of them late night telly programmes, the type my Alf tunes into accidentally when he's looking for something on Sky. At least that's what he tells me, and he still thinks I believe him, daft old beggar.

The reader should hopefully be getting the idea that the narrator is, despite her protestations of innocence, very nosey indeed. She is desperate to know what goes on in other people's lives and probably has a pretty dull life herself. After all, she has time to look on the internet for a padlock picking website!

Is there a place for monologues in short story writing?

I think there is – yes – not least because it gives us a way of really getting into a character's head. Writing a monologue basically means the narrator is talking in the voice of the character. Monologues are a brilliant tool for developing characters' voices and making them different.

What is pace?

Pace is one of the hardest aspects of writing to define. It's also one of the hardest things to get right. Or so I find. So what actually is pace? Well, if you start with the idea that it's a rate of progress, you won't go far wrong.

In writing terms it's the rate of progress at which your story unfolds. But what is the optimum pace? This, of course, depends on what you're writing. A very short story, of 1000 words or less, demands that you start off running. Or at least go straight in at some point of conflict. There is no time to hang about. During a longer short story you may have time for a slower scene. You certainly can't go flat out for too long without exhausting the readers. Neither can you go too slowly, for fear they'll lose interest or fall asleep.

How do you create pace?

Well, on a technical level you do it with language: the shorter the sentences, the faster the pace. If you're writing a tense fast-paced scene, then keeping your sentences short (even down to as little as one word) will do a great deal to move things along.

The same applies to the words you use. Keep the language simple. For example, if you're describing a chase scene, there's no time for long descriptions of the scenery your protagonists are passing. They wouldn't have time to notice (viewpoint) and the reader doesn't want the action held up. You still need glimpses of setting – naturally they can't run through a vacuum – but keep it snappy and you'll maintain pace.

On a more general level, character introspection slows pace. Dialogue speeds it up. What you really need is balance, or your writing swiftly becomes one-dimensional and without depth.

Plot and pace

A short story plot, by its nature, needs to be kept fairly simple. There isn't enough room for it to be complicated. Generally a short story plot will tend to focus on a single event or theme.

Number of characters

A short story of a thousand words almost certainly won't have more than two or three characters, one of whom will be the main character. There is a lot more room for characters in a three or four thousand word story, but whatever you are writing your characters must be essential to the plot.

Timescale

A short story will tend to have a very short timescale, often only a few hours in time, although, as we've already discovered, flashback will often be used to recreate the past. However, it's possible using certain types of structure to take your characters over much longer periods.

Tips from the experts

Celia Bryce says:

'When I have an idea, it's a matter of getting it down as quickly as possible, warts and all. From then a story grows out of it, undergoing many, many, changes (tenses, viewpoint, person, even conflict) until it feels right. Structurally, I want the story to begin at or just before the point of conflict and end with that conflict resolved, not necessarily happily, but at least with a sense of hope. I like to alter pace and mood by using flashback, exploring what has happened in the past, its relevance to the present. This all takes time. It can be frustrating. However I learn something from every story I write, every story I read, every story I listen to. There's always some stone unturned.'

Chapter Ten

Putting It All Together

Why do I need an attention grabbing opening paragraph?

The opening paragraph is the first thing the editor sees. If it doesn't grab her attention she may not read any further. In fact, I was once told by an editor that when she was choosing stories to buy she first read the opening paragraph. If she liked that she read the closing paragraph and if she liked that, she read the middle.

If you are entering a short-story competition it is also vital to catch the judge or first reader's attention. As anyone who has judged a short-story competition will know, it's hard work being a judge. Judges are busy people and are often fitting in judging between their own writing commitments.

I've judged a lot of writing competitions myself and when I'm faced with a pile of manuscripts, it's the title and opening paragraph which dictate which manuscripts I'll read first. For readers who are often required to sift through dozens, or even hundreds, of manuscripts then it's even more vital to get your manuscript to stand out. Having an absolutely brilliant opening paragraph will help.

There are several techniques you can use to make

sure your opening paragraph is attention grabbing. Below are some of them.

Ways of hooking your reader

- Throw the reader straight into the action by starting with a piece of dialogue.
- Introduce at least one character. Readers want to read about characters, not long pieces of description.
- Set up a question in the reader's mind. One way of doing this is to begin with your character in an intriguing situation so the reader will want to read on to find out what happens next.
- If you can, try also to give some sense of setting or atmosphere that will set the tone of the piece.
- Use a style appropriate for what you are writing. Short sentences build tension. Longer ones indicate a slower start.

Some brilliant opening paragraphs

With the Best of Intentions by Teresa Ashby, published in *Woman's Weekly Fiction Special*

> *I knocked on Mrs Allison's door with every intention of robbing her. Shocked? I thought you might be. And if I tell you that Mrs Allison is my great-grandmother, I expect you'll be even more shocked.*

Don't Do It, Molly! by Steve Beresford, published in *Take A Break Fiction Feast*

> *Molly Breckham had never been at all inclined to believe in anything that was remotely paranormal or otherworldly until Ralph turned up in her bedroom just before 3am on a Wednesday morning.*

"I wouldn't do that if I were you," Ralph said.

Kill Phil by Jan Wright, published in *The Weekly News*

As Phil started to run, I grabbed a size 12 Doc Marten and tried to flatten him. "Die, die, die," I yelled, as I struck a blow for every time my boyfriend had stood me up, let me down and lied to me.

Sweet Scent of Memories by Adam Millward, published in *My Weekly*

Today was always going to be hard. I'd have been kidding myself if I'd ever thought otherwise. Twenty-five years of marriage and my husband struggles to remember my name, let alone to buy a present.

How could you not read on after opening paragraphs like these?

These openings all put a question into the reader's mind. There is some kind of problem, something is happening and we know about it instantly. They all involve people. We join the story at a moment of change. They are all intriguing enough to make us want to read on. In short, they all act as a hook.

So, now we know how to do it, I think it's worth a look at how not to do it. Just as there are things you should do in your opening paragraph, there are things you should try and avoid.

Some terrible opening paragraphs

Example one

Tanya, Liz and Joanne were sisters. Tanya was the eldest by three years. Liz was the middle

91

sister and Joanne was the youngest. Their
mother Claire loved having daughters. She
loved dressing them up and taking them to ballet
and horse riding and swimming. Tanya was the
best swimmer, although Liz wasn't bad, but
Joanne was much slower. Peter, their father,
said she'd catch up in time..

Everyone got that?

Introducing too many characters is confusing. If your reader has to go back to work out who is who, she will very likely give up.

Don't introduce all your characters at once. Focus on one or two until the reader is sufficiently interested in them to want to carry on reading.

Example two

It was a very dull day in Dorset. It was raining
in fact, quite heavily. The clouds were grey and
the sky was grey and the streets were grey.
There were quite a few puddles. It was
miserable and it was cold and it was very, very
dull. The sun hadn't been out all day. In some
places the drains were starting to fill up,
possibly blocked by leaves, possibly just
struggling with so much rain.

I should think that most readers would be struggling by now, too, as it isn't just the weather that's dull. This opening paragraph is repetitive and boring and vaguely depressing. And who wants to read about the rain? Mind you, it would probably be just as boring if it was a beautiful sunny day and I'd written reams of description about that.

Too much description of any kind may well switch your reader off in a short story, particularly in the opening paragraph. Don't start with a long piece of scene setting unless it is absolutely essential to your story and even then it would probably be better if any scene-setting were done through the eyes of the main character.

The rule here is that something must be happening. And it's probably best not to open with a description of the weather unless it's critical for mood.

Example three

> *Lisa loved her job on the checkout at Whites Supermarket. She was pretty sure she was going to get promoted soon. Her boss, Wendy, had said as much on this morning's tea break, despite the small misunderstanding there had been with the till takings yesterday. That hadn't really been Lisa's fault; she'd been rather tied up with the old woman who'd collapsed in Aisle Three. Aisle Three wasn't actually hers, but she'd had to get involved being a First Aider. She was really glad she was a First Aider, although if it weren't for John she probably wouldn't have had the confidence. She'd been so much more self confident since they met. He was very supportive and made her feel good about herself. He'd been the one who'd suggested she go for the promotion, shortly after he'd been promoted at the bowling alley. Wendy had been promoted too.*

This story lacks focus. What is it actually about? Is it about Lisa's job, Lisa's relationship, the till takings, the old lady? It could perhaps be about all of these things, but they shouldn't all be introduced in the first paragraph.

Don't give too much information too soon. Too much information can make the narrative very dense and difficult to read.

How do I write good opening paragraphs?

I think the key here is practice. For me, opening paragraphs are so important that I often write them in isolation. I will set myself a timer and write a page or so of opening paragraphs. Writing opening paragraphs without worrying about how your story will progress is wonderfully liberating. I recommend it.

However, I'd also like to add a word of warning here. If you do have a story idea in mind and are sitting down to write the whole thing, then my advice is not to worry too much about the opening paragraph until you've completed the story. This may sound like a contradiction, but there's a danger of spending so long perfecting the opening paragraph that you never actually get any further.

Perfecting the opening paragraph can be done last.

How do I know if my opening paragraph works?

Once you have finished the story, re-read the first paragraph in isolation and ask yourself if it's intriguing enough to make someone else want to read on. If possible, read it to a writer friend and ask him or her. If necessary, rewrite it.

How to maintain your middle

So, you have written a catchy opening that is sure to get an editor's or judge's attention. How do you develop it from there? The answer lies in what you have written so far. Look at the opening paragraphs as the set-up of your story. You have so far (hopefully) got the following:

1) One or more characters.
2) A moment of change or problem – if there is no moment of change or problem, you possibly haven't got a story to develop and you may need to rethink your opening.

The development of character and problem (also known as plot) is what happens next, I'll demonstrate exactly how this works with one of my own short stories. Here's the opening of A Perfect Match, published in a *Woman's Weekly Fiction Special*:

> *Nick Munroe was not in the habit of finding stilettos in his bed. Or to be more precise, one stiletto, red, with what his daughter, Chloe, would have called a killer heel. He turned it over in his hand and he couldn't stop himself from wondering what the owner of such a shoe might be like.*
>
> *Someone young, that was for sure. He imagined she would be blonde too – and leggy. He'd noticed of late that all sorts of women – even tall ones – wore high heels. Well, at least the ones on television did.*

On the surface, this story is about a character who finds a shoe in his bed and wonders who it might belong to – it's a little like a Cinderella opening from the viewpoint of Prince Charming. But of course the story needs to be about much more than that.

The next question it might be pertinent to ask yourself, if you haven't done so already, is what is your story really about?

Nick Munroe's real problem is that he hasn't got

over the loss of his wife. A shy farmer, he doesn't know how to relate to other people, particularly women, and move on. He is too embarrassed to confront the tour leader, M, and ask her about the shoe. So, continuing with the Cinderella theme, what he actually does is to keep the red stiletto and surreptitiously study the women on board to see if he can work out if it belongs to any of them. He decides to tell his daughter about it.

That night he phoned Chloe to see how they were coping.

"Everything's cool, Dad. We're fine. How's it going? Met any interesting women yet?"

He told her about the stiletto, his voice light and matter of fact, as if it were an everyday occurrence.

"Well, you could go round with it on a silver pillow and ask all the women on board to try it on and see who it fits. Maybe it's fate, Dad. Maybe it's the route to finding the next Mrs Monroe."

"I doubt that." He was startled that his daughter's thoughts were running so close to his own. "It's probably been left behind, I'm sure if it belonged to anyone on board, they'd have mentioned it by now."

"Well, you could try asking them." There was laughter in Chloe's voice. "One stiletto's not much good on its own, is it? If it were mine, I'd want it back, pronto."

He hung up, feeling guilty. She was right. He was being ridiculous.

He took it to breakfast, in a plastic carrier, which seemed more discreet than just strolling in, dangling it by its strap. After coffee, he managed to catch M alone.

"I found this in my accommodation. It doesn't belong to me." Well that was pretty obvious. "I thought you might be able to return it to its rightful owner."

"Thanks, love. Course I will." She peeked into the bag, oblivious to his discomfort. "My word, that's a beauty, isn't it? Wonder who's lost it."

For the rest of the morning he was on tenterhooks, he wasn't sure why. After all, there was no reason why M should even tell him who had lost the shoe.

All this fuss over a shoe. Well, at least coming on this trip had taught him one thing, he needed to get back into the swing of life. He needed to do things, meet people, take an interest in the world outside his farm.

So the middle of your story should develop the character's problem you initially set up. Because you have started at a moment of change, you now need to fill the reader in on some details. How your characters have got to this point and what exactly is going on here.

In Nick's case the superficial problem – the discovery of the stiletto – is easily resolved, he simply hands it over to M. But the resolution of his real problem, his shyness and his inability to move on since his wife died, takes a little more development.

To summarise: whatever you are writing, your middle section is likely to include the following:

Some explanation of how the character has got to this point, shown via flashback and dialogue.

A deepening of characterisation.

Some hint of how the characters are going to resolve the situation.

How to write the perfect ending

In the last section we talked about the development of the middle of a story. We developed our story by letting the reader know a little more about the characters and their problems, using any flashback we needed to illustrate. Now, we have to bring our piece to a satisfying conclusion.

This, in my experience, is the hardest bit. But once again, the answer lies in what you have already written. What strands have you set up so far, and exactly what are you trying to say?

Let's go back to A Perfect Match. Here's an extract from later in the story:

> *It wasn't until the last night that Nick found out who the red stiletto belonged to – and by then he'd almost forgotten its existence. He'd enjoyed this break more than he'd thought possible. He'd grown used to the rhythm of the boat and having time just to enjoy the views. But most of all, he'd grown used to having M around.*

So Nick has got over his shyness and he's rather keen on M in a quiet sort of way. So he is learning to move on. He has almost forgotten the red stiletto, his superficial problem, but the reader does of course need to know who it belongs to. If the reader didn't find out, the ending wouldn't be satisfactory.

Here's how this strand of the story comes to a close.

> *"Oh, by the way, I found out who that shoe belonged to," she said, as she sat next to him for*

the farewell meal.

"That's good news," he murmured, wondering how he could ever have thought her unapproachable.

"It belongs to my son's girlfriend – I'd lent them the boat for a party just before this trip." She rested her elbow alongside his. "I'd told them not to go in the cabins – out of interest where did you find it?"

"Just inside the door," Nick said without a flicker. "Must have been dropped from a bag, maybe?"

"Hmm." Her lips twitched and he could see she didn't believe a word.

So Nick is proving himself to be a nice man by not revealing where he really found the shoe.

These are the closing paragraphs of the story:

They were the last to leave the galley, and just before he got up, he took a deep breath and he said. "Tell me if I'm talking out of turn, but is there any chance you'd have dinner with me some time?"

"I'd like that very much." Her face dimpled in the candlelight. "Nick – I should tell you what the M stands for, shouldn't I?"

"I can't pretend I haven't been curious."

"It's Marilyn." Her dimples increased as she spoke, and he wondered if she remembered what his surname was. Probably – that would explain her quiet amusement.

His heart fluttered like a boy's as he said goodnight.

In the privacy of his cabin, he phoned Chloe

and told her he was going on a date.

"Well, don't get too serious, Dad. You won't be able to marry her. You can't land her with a name like Marilyn Monroe."

But Nick's thoughts were far away from marriage. They were far away from red stilettos too. It was nice to be back in the swing of life, listening to the quiet lapping of water against the boat and knowing that tomorrow he'd be back on solid ground – in more ways than one.

So, to summarise: your ending should bring the subject to a close in a satisfactory way. If you are writing fiction, you may have a twist. If you have a twist it should neatly bring the strands of the story together, and also surprise the reader.

If you don't have a twist, you may have a harder job on your hands because you have to leave the readers feeling satisfied without having surprised them. And you need to do this without being too predictable. This is where a universal truth comes in handy.

Personally, I find that writing the perfect end is the hardest part of writing a story. But it's important to persevere until you've got it.

Before we leave this section, let's have a quick look at what not to do.

Bad endings
- Are predictable – the reader can guess from the outset what the ending will be.
- They cheat the reader, i.e. everything that happened was in fact a dream.
- They leave the reader feeling let down.

Good endings
- Round up the story neatly, although it's not always

necessary to tie up every loose end.

- If you're writing a twist ending, then your conclusion must have been sufficiently signposted, earlier in the story, without the reader guessing what it is.
- A good ending is often tied up with the beginning. Perhaps some question raised earlier is answered in a way that the reader didn't expect.
- If you're writing a magazine story then the ending must also be upbeat or hopeful.

Ways of getting it right

Write the ending first. This is especially pertinent if you're writing a twist. It's not failsafe, though. In my experience, my story has often changed so much that by the time I get to the end, it no longer fits and I have to think again.

The clue to your ending is very often in whatever you've already written. Ask yourself what your story is about. Not just on the surface, but what it is *really* about. This is often the key to your ending, which should underline whatever point you're trying to make.

Here are some examples of the "What is it really about" method.

Example one

On the surface, my story Straight Lines, published in *Woman's Weekly*, is about a couple holidaying in Italy.

It is *really* about the woman's unease that she and her husband don't seem to have much in common. He is practical and sensible, she is idealistic and dreamy. This is the end.

We sit and sip Chianti in the sun and look at the hillside opposite. The fields are a patchwork of

101

ochre and gold squares. Winding paths lead up to red-roofed farmhouses, just visible between the cypress trees.

Straight lines and curves, I think idly, blending together to make up the whole picture. They could exist without each other, of course, but a world made up of one or the other wouldn't have the same balance, the same beauty. As I lean back into Mark's arms, I think with sudden insight, that a world without both would actually – like the ruins we've been walking around all week – be only half complete.

Example two

At first glance, another of my stories, Rolling Down Hillsides, published in *Woman's Weekly*, is about a woman's anxiousness that her new boyfriend won't tell her how old he is (he's much younger than she is) and they are going away for the first time.

It is really about the fact that you have to take risks in love, whatever your age is.

"You have to take risks sometimes, Linda." His eyes are serious and I know he's not talking about hills. "If it's really important," he adds softly: "I'll risk telling you how old I am and you can decide if I'm likely to mean more than a pleasant summer fling."

"You mean more than that already," I say before I have time to think that he might only want a fling. It's too late to take the words back, but as I look into his face I see with a growing warmth that it was the right thing to say. He

draws me into his arms and we kiss easily – as easily as we laugh.

Later, we both agree that nothing in life is risk free, but there are some things that feel so right that the risk is worth taking.

Example three

On the surface, my story My Gran, published in *Woman's Weekly*, is about a character making the effort to visit her old gran, however tired she is.

It is *really* about memories in the making.

Today it was a huge effort, but I enjoy these times as much as she does. Not just for the old memories, I reflect, but for the new ones we're making now.

A patchwork quilt of memories, all sewn together on a Friday afternoon in Gran's warm lounge. Memories, which, perhaps, are all the more precious, because she's not my real Gran. I was one of her brood of temporary foster children. She couldn't have her own, but she looked after dozens of other people's kids all her life. She gave me all the security and love that my own mother wasn't emotionally equipped to do.

I smile as I drive. I have a feeling that in years to come when Gran's no longer around – because no one lives forever – I'll be able to get out my patchwork quilt of memories and look at it. And that it'll grow more dazzling – because memories are like that, aren't they?

Untouchable. Set in sunlight. So˙ that years after they were made, we can still feel their

warmth.
   No matter how cold the day.

What to do if your ending falls flat

If you have the slightest doubt that your ending isn't all it could be – and I think most writers err on the side of self-critical so you'll probably know – don't send it out.

If you're not sure, then enlist the help of a writer friend or writing group, who know what you're trying to achieve.

If it isn't working, do it again. Keep writing endings until you hit on the right one.

I've been doing this for so long that my instincts are pretty good. I know when I've written a good ending – I get at worst a feeling of satisfaction and at best a tingle down my back.

Sometimes I suspect that I haven't written such a good ending, but I've been wrestling with it for so long – and I know there are writers out there who know exactly what I mean about wrestling with endings – that I just think, oh hang it (or words to that effect) and send it out anyway. It is always a mistake. The story usually comes back.

Often if your ending isn't working, the answer is in what you've already written.

With practice, it's possible to see where you've gone wrong and you may need to delete back to that point and start again.

I liken it to a dropped stitch in a piece of knitting. You need to unravel back to that point and start afresh to make the whole piece work.

Tips from the experts

Ian Burton says:

'Writing fiction is like planting seeds in the garden except that the seed packets are blank so you have no idea what's going to come up. But as time goes by it becomes more apparent. On that basis, it's best not to worry about the ending of your story until you get there or at least closer to it. After all the ending can only grow out of what has gone before.

Endings are not something you can practice in isolation as you can with say dialogue or characterization. But there is one practical thing you can do which will help your endings and that is to look carefully at how films, novels, short stories end. Why did they end there?

There are some endings which are just so right it's hard to imagine that there could ever have been any doubt. Legend has it that the ending of Casablanca was changed so many times that even the actors weren't sure until the day of shooting. But it was not the expected ending and it is often said that if Rick and Ilsa had ended up 'the happy couple' it would not have been such a memorable film. But it's still an 'of course' ending – Rick's love of Ilsa compels him to do the right thing.

If Tony and Maria had jumped on a bus and got away from New York City... no, it's not really on, is it?

If what was left of the Magnificent Seven had settled down and started to plough fields and raise crops...

I'm often quoting Robert McKee, Hollywood script guru who says – "always give the audience what they expect but not in the way that they expect it."

So, if you're unsure what your story ending will be –
it might help to think first of what the reader is
expecting but then add a slightly unexpected spin to it.'

Chapter Eleven

Cutting and Editing

Murder your darlings

'Murder your darlings' was a phrase I heard a lot when I was learning to write. I was told it meant I had to cut all superfluous words and phrases from what I was writing, and that they'd often be the words and phrases I liked best.

It sounds awful, doesn't it, and it is awful cutting out what you often feel are the best bits of your work. So why do we have to do it? Well, as I've gone further along my writing journey, I've realised that cutting almost always improves writing. I write short stories and I don't have room for self-indulgence. The fact that I like or am proud of a particular phrase is not a good enough reason for leaving it in.

But all is not lost. If your beautiful phrase is essential to the story, then by all means leave it in – but be strict with yourself. Is it really essential? Is it moving along the plot? Is it developing the character? Is it actually in character viewpoint, or is it really authorial voice, i.e. are you throwing in the line because you think it's good writing?

If you've asked yourself these questions and are

honest about the answers and the phrase does indeed have to come out, then all is still not lost. Keep a separate document and move the phrase into it for future use. One day, you'll have the perfect place for it.

This is actually one of the best tips I know for any cutting and editing. If you are cutting chunks of a story because your version is, for example, 500 words over the length it needs to be to fit the market, then just move the chunk – for now – to another document. If I'm working on a story saved on my computer as Changing Places, then anything I cut out of it will be saved as another file called Bits of Changing Places.

The beauty of this system is that it's pain-free. I know I haven't lost anything. If indeed I later decide I've cut the wrong chunk of a story, I can put it back. It continually amazes me that this hardly ever happens. My finished versions are tighter, better and stronger for the cut, and I am a writer who tends to underwrite, not overwrite.

For me, the moral of this story is that my writing always benefits from a cut. Try it on yours, you may be pleasantly surprised.

Are edits essential?

There are some well-established writers who say that edits are not essential – if we can write then we shouldn't have to do it twice. We should, with practice, get it right first time.

For me, this is the same as saying I write perfectly. I know I do not. I don't do anything perfectly, however much practice I have. I've been practising writing daily for the last twenty years and I have yet to perfect the art. My final drafts are not perfect either. It means I'm human. So, to my mind, edits are essential, and most writers don't do enough of them.

How many drafts should I write?

I think this is a question that only you can answer. I don't believe in writing by numbers, i.e. sticking to a fixed set of rules. Writing is an art form. When you are experienced your own instincts will guide you. In the meantime it's probably better to do more drafts than you think you need.

Is it possible to over edit?

At the risk of contradicting myself, then I'd say, yes it is. Our first work tends to be a splurge of words that pour out – well they pour out on a good day! On a bad day it might feel more like pulling teeth with no anaesthetic. First drafts have a rawness about them and hopefully a sparkle. And I think that it's possible to take this sparkle out with too much editing.

I've seen writers who have actually managed to polish all the sparkle away from their original piece, leaving a final draft that is flat and rather emotionless. Please be careful – but in the final analysis you'll have to trust your instincts about when enough is enough. This gets much easier with time and experience.

What should I look for when I edit?

Repetition

For me, the number one fault in first drafts is repetition. I often repeat myself when I write a first draft, both in meaning and with words. I don't know whether it's the way my brain works, but I'll very often find I've repeated a word either in the same paragraph or in the one below. It's almost as if my writing brain is saying:

'That's a good word; we'll have another one of those, shall we?'

I also have favourite words. You'll have your own, but these are some of mine: just; quite; suddenly; that; and bit. I sometimes use the word search facility to go through and delete these words in my final edit.

Another way of repetition is to say the same thing in a different way.

> *And standing there in the sun, on that dusty afternoon Pam realised she'd never felt quite so happy in her life, which wasn't all that surprising when she thought about it. Pottering around a car boot sale was one of her favourite ways to spend a Sunday morning.*

These two sentences are both telling us that Pam is happy. Only one of them is needed, although in the end I discarded both in favour of showing Pam being happy rather than directly telling the reader.

Overused punctuation

I'm also rather fond of dashes – I litter them through my work – and it's a difficult habit to break. You'll find plenty besides the two in this paragraph that I've put in deliberately.

A good rule is that less is more. Be sparing with exclamation marks. They tend to be very visible.

Telling when you've already shown

This is effectively another form of repetition. There is no need to show the readers something and then tell them as well.

For example, *Tears streamed down Laura's face. She was very unhappy.*

What about adverbs?

Fashions change, but I am of the opinion that adverbs should be used sparingly. They tend to weaken writing, rather than strengthen it. If possible use a strong verb instead. For example, instead of saying, *he ran quickly*, try *he raced*.

Have a look at these pieces of writing.

Example one

> *The door slammed loudly and Nick groaned, equally loudly. They'd had such a good marriage once. How had things gone so dreadfully wrong? He couldn't even remember when it had started to happen. The rot had crept into their marriage like a cancer, so slowly, so insidiously, he hadn't been aware of it at first. But he could no longer pretend everything was fine. He absolutely had to find a way to make Claire talk to him.*
>
> *He got up and went cautiously to the window. Her car was gone, he saw bleakly. How long, this time, before she came back? How long would it be, he thought despairingly, before she'd finally admit that her refusal to talk to him was slowly destroying their love?*

I make that twelve. Not bad for 125 words. Do they strengthen the text or weaken it?

Perhaps before we can answer this, we need to see which ones can be removed without altering the meaning of the piece. If a word can be removed (any word, not just an adverb) without altering the meaning of a piece of writing, then it has to be superfluous. Doesn't it?

Example two

> *The door slammed and Nick groaned. They'd*
> *had such a good marriage once. How had things*
> *gone so wrong? He couldn't even remember*
> *when it had started to happen. The rot had crept*
> *into their marriage like a cancer. He hadn't*
> *been aware of it at first. But he could no longer*
> *pretend everything was fine. He had to find a*
> *way to make Claire talk to him.*
>
> *He got up and went to the window. Her car*
> *was gone. How long, this time, before she came*
> *back? How long would it be, he thought, before*
> *she'd admit that her refusal to talk to him was*
> *destroying their love?*

So, none of them are *actually* necessary, but does that mean none of them should be there? Why then, were adverbs invented in the first place? Perhaps, like all writing, there's a balance. If you're in doubt, take a highlighter pen to your work. Use it to highlight all adverbs and then go through it and see how many of them can be removed or replaced with a strong verb without weakening the story. As an exercise try allowing yourself one adverb per thousand words. This is tough, but it's amazing how much it can improve your writing.

Why are clichés a problem?

Most clichés came into being because they were the perfect way to say something. So why change them?

The answer to this, I think, is that anything we hear too often is less meaningful – after a while it loses its meaning, and hence its impact, altogether.

They will certainly not make your writing original.

These are two good reasons to try and avoid them.

Here are some of the clichés that annoy me the most – you will no doubt be able to add to the list.

- She awoke with a start
- She was white as a sheet
- Her legs felt like jelly
- A split second
- His heart beat like a drum

It's actually quite good fun to see if you can get a twist on a cliché. What I mean by a twist is to just alter the words slightly, so the cliché is still recognisable, but not quite the same.

For example, these are some replacements for the clichés above:

- She jerked awake
- She was hospital sheet white (assuming the hospital context worked)
- Her legs jellied beneath her
- A split of a second (supplied by Ian Burton)
- He heard nothing above the drum of his heart

I spend quite a lot of time – when I'm not actually writing – seeing if I can think up new ways of saying very familiar things. The best way I've found of doing this, incidentally, is to make a mental note when I'm experiencing an emotion or situation. One of the wonderful things about being a writer is that nothing you see, hear or feel is ever wasted.

Should all clichés be removed?

They are fine when used in dialogue – after all, we tend to talk in clichés, don't we? But again, be careful.

If all your characters talk in the same clichés then you are probably not writing very good dialogue. For a start your characters will all have the same voice.

Here are some examples of writers using new and original ways to replace clichéd phrases and similes:

> *'The blood in my veins ran hot and heavy like liquid lead.'*

From, A Box Marked Secret by Rachel Lovell
Published in *Woman's Weekly Fiction Special*.

> *'There were fireworks and water canons and a welcoming fleet of little boats clustered around the ship like cygnets around a mother swan.'*

From, Bring Back a Penguin by Jill Butcher
Published in *Woman's Weekly Fiction Special*.

> *'The television had a thousand channels and her CD Collection was as high as the Eiffel Tower.'*

From, Let Me Spoil You by Lynne Hackles
Published in *Take A Break*

> *'Where the lamplight caught the dome of his head, it glimmered like a polished egg.'*

From, You're Living a Bad Life by Geraldine Ryan.
Published in *Take A Break*.

Tips from the experts

Linda Mitchelmore says:

'I was advised to be mindful of the words I chose right at the beginning of my short-story writing career. Just because a story is short doesn't mean you have to scrimp on words. Get into the habit of being specific about colour – never red, but carmine, scarlet, pillar-box, rosehip, blood, burgundy and so on; each will count as one word but will bring an image more alive to the reader. And the same goes for all the other colours too. And make movement actually move – not just walk, but amble, stroll, saunter, run, rush, sprint and so on.'

Chapter Twelve,

Titles

What should a title do?

A title should fit your story and should give a hint of what it's about. A title should also intrigue the reader and make her want to read on to find out what happens.

A good title can also work on more than one level. It may have one meaning before you read the story and a second meaning after you've read it. For example, I once wrote a story called Changing Places. It was about an old lady, Annie, going back to the cottage where she'd lived as a small girl and finding a new house in its place. This was the first meaning.

As the story progressed, Annie went on to have a conversation with the small girl who now lived there. By the time the reader reached the end of the story she would have discovered that the title also referred to Annie putting herself in the child's place, i.e. she was changing places with the child – albeit only in her head!

What should a title not do?

A title should not give away the end of your story, for example, The Rescue Dog That Saved us from the Fire, or, The Old Lady who Turned Out to be a Crook. These are rather over the top examples, but you see my point. Incidentally, these titles would probably be perfect for a feature.

Some writers have no problems at all thinking up brilliant titles. Sadly I'm not one of them. I struggle over titles. It sometimes takes me as long to find a title as it does to write the story in the first place.

Are there any short cuts to finding a good title?

Yes, I think there are. Over the years I have come up with some title tactics that have helped me. These are some of them:

Echo the theme in your title
- Priorities
- Lost
- Chocolate
- Late

Use well known phrases
- Playing Away
- A Game of Chance
- Tempting Fate
- The Language of Flowers

Borrow well known titles from songs or films
- Brief Encounter
- Room with a View
- Stairway to Heaven

Use titles that play on words
- Auld Fang Syne (credit where credit's due, a fellow writer thought this one up for me, thank you, David Kendrick)
- Four Fathers and a Wedding

- The Day After Yesterday

Use alliteration
- Bridges and Butterflies
- Love and Lingonberry Juice
- Perfect Posers

Use words that wouldn't normally go together
- Blue Milkshake Sky
- The Fridge Man and the Dancers
- Polar Bears and Hair Extensions

Proverbs, or parts of proverbs, make good titles
- For richer for poorer
- The food of love

If all else fails it might be possible to use a line of dialogue or a line from your story as a title. At times I've been known to put a line of dialogue in – just so I can use it as a title!

Here are some interesting facts about titles:
There is no copyright on titles, which is great for short-story writing as you can use the same title over and over again.

Even if you do think up a brilliant title there is no guarantee it won't be changed to something else when your piece is published. This won't happen in a competition, but it might happen if you're published in magazines or broadcast.

I was once told by a magazine editor that as far as he was concerned I could forget about titles and just number my stories, as it was their policy to change titles anyway. I didn't take him up on it, needless to say.

Title tip

Carry a notebook around with you and jot down titles when they occur to you. Then when you need a title, flick through and see if you can find one. Even better – why not write a story to fit the title?

Tips from the experts

Joyce Begg says:

'As regards thinking up titles, I find there are various routes. Sometimes a well known phrase, or a song title, can inspire the story to start with, e.g. 'Someone To Watch Over Me.' But usually I try to think of a title that reflects the essence of whatever story I'm writing. Sometimes it's quite simple, like the story published one January which I called 'White Wedding', and which was set in the deep snows of 1947. So the wedding was 'white' on two counts. (The hero – on a tractor – collects his bride from a snowed-in cottage. This was based on what really happened to one of our village ladies.) Then there was 'Seizing the Moment', which was about a girl who worked in a small café/restaurant, and who took advantage of her boss's holiday to make improvements to the menu. She really did seize the moment, changed lots of things, and found herself in hot water – though in the end she was proved right and the boss finally approved. I had another story, published one Easter, which was called 'The Chocolate Shop', since that was the place where all the action took place. Not only that, but the hero, an artist, painted a picture of the shop itself, so it was central to absolutely everything.

I would suggest that a writer should choose a title that focuses on what really matters in your story, reflecting the feelings or situation or actions of the characters. It should lead the readers in, and invite them to be part of the story.'

I asked these magazine editors the question: when submitting stories for publication, do titles matter?

Gaynor Davies, fiction editor of *Woman's Weekly*, says:

'Not really because we change them if we don't like them! They certainly matter to the readers, though, as they're what entices them in.'

Angela Gilchrist, editor of *The People's Friend*, says:

'Titles don't matter at all! We frequently change them in any case because they have to fit with all the other material being included in the magazine that week. Also, the illustration chosen to go with the story may require a particular approach that the original title just doesn't cover. We're looking at the whole package – title, write up, illustration, byline – whereas the author only ever sees the original text.'

Chapter Thirteen

Incorporating Life Into Fiction

Fiction means that you make everything up – correct? Well, actually no. At the risk of sticking my head above the parapet and being shot down in flames – lovely mixed metaphor there, I'd say there is an element of fiction in every non-fiction piece, and an element of reality in every piece of fiction.

After all, where else do ideas, characters and plots come from – if not life?

My fiction, and that of many other writers who I've asked about this, tends to be a composite of reality and imagination. I actually see fiction as being like a piece of knitting (not that I knit) where I incorporate elements of reality mixed together with imagination.

I might use a real name (excluding surname). I might use a real piece of dialogue, a real physical description, or a real character trait but if they all came from the same person, I'd put them into different stories.

This is for two reasons:

1) I'd hate to upset anybody.
2) Reality does not translate very well into fiction.

Real life events offer great opportunities for fiction

writers, but can rarely be used verbatim. Reality is littered with inconsistencies, loose ends and red herrings. Reality often appears to have no meaning or message and it certainly doesn't have a convenient end.

Short stories should have these elements – at least in part.

The beauty of fiction, I've always thought, is that while your story may begin in reality, for the reasons already stated the ending is usually made up.

However, real life is a great starting point for fiction. Here are some of the ways in which I borrow from life.

Using dialogue from life

Snippets of conversation are a great starting point. Here are some lines I've been lucky enough to overhear and use in fiction, although not necessarily in their original form:

"If you see a 5 foot blackbird in a tree, it's mine."

"One day I'm going to open a pub for people over seventy and call it The Crinkly Arms."

"Thursdays are the new Fridays."

"I only need to have two drinks and I'm taking my clothes off."

They were all manna from heaven and they all sparked off ideas for short stories. I find that overhearing a snippet, as opposed to the whole conversation, is actually better because you can let your imagination run riot.

Using real people as characters

For obvious reasons I would advise against using a real person in a story – but it is fine to use bits of real people. For example, if I happened to meet a six foot three firefighter called Jed, with black hair, blue eyes and a slightly too-big nose he felt self-conscious about, who played the guitar in his spare time and was a first class chef, then I might use elements of his character, but I wouldn't transport him whole. Actually, thinking about it, I might be tempted to run off with him, rather than write about him, but don't tell my husband!

Seriously though, here's how I might transfer Jed into a story. I might write about an office worker who was a first class chef and whose dream was to own his own restaurant. Or I might call my next hero, Jed. Or I might give my next hero black hair, blue eyes and a slightly too big nose. Or I might write about a firefighter. But I would keep these elements separate.

What if someone recognises him or herself?

It is highly unlikely this will happen. We rarely see ourselves as others see us. In my experience it's far more likely to happen the other way round. My mum for example occasionally reads my stories and will comment, "I know who you based that character on". She has, to date, always been completely wrong.

However, do not use real names. It isn't often necessary to use surnames in short stories, but if you do, then make sure they aren't real people. Not always possible, I know, but be aware of this. The last thing you want to do is to upset someone – or get yourself sued.

Can I use the bad bits of someone's personality?

One of the wonderful things about writing is that you can get your own back. The miserable man, who swore at you for going in through the exit of the car park instead of the entrance, can be the baddie in your next story, where he will of course come to a sticky end. Yippee!

A much more sophisticated revenge than shouting and swearing back at him, I'm sure you'll agree!

Using real events as plots

I'm afraid I can't help myself here – it is part of my writer's make up. No one is safe. My friends' and family's problems, dramas and secrets, will all eventually be incorporated into fiction. There is one exception – I won't write anything that I know would hurt someone if it appeared in print – however well it was disguised. I can't guarantee that I won't ever write about it in the future, but I blame my subconscious for this.

A good source of storylines can come from newspapers, particularly the quirky human interest stories. I'd like to add a word of warning here, too. I tend to avoid very big or high profile storylines, partly because I don't want to profit from other people's pain and partly because lots of writers may well try the same storylines so they will quickly become a familiar theme.

Using emotions

I do find that while we don't all suffer from the same problems, we all have the same feelings. We've all felt afraid, excited, alone, devastated, overwhelmed, anxious – need I go on? It's often possible to transfer emotions between similar situations. For example, you might not know what it's like to have been rejected by someone you really admired, but you may very well know what it's like to be rejected by an employer for a job or promotion you really wanted. The sense of failure will be the same.

Or you might not have your own children, so in theory can't understand maternal love, but you may have had a much loved pet.

When I'm writing about a problem of which I've had no experience, I'll either try to imagine how I'd feel in that character's shoes, or I'll ask someone who has been through the event or problem themselves.

It's very important to get character motivation and psychology right. If it isn't right, it won't ring true for the readers and they may stop reading.

Using real places

There are various schools of thought on this – my own feeling is that it's rather nice to use real places if we're talking big, for example, a city such as London, or a landmark such as the New Forest or Corfe Castle, or even a beach. But if I do use a real place I try to avoid being too specific about where my characters go exactly.

If my characters visited the New Forest and went to a coffee shop or pub, then I'd avoid using the name of a real coffee shop or pub in the New Forest. That doesn't mean you can't use the details of a real place, just don't name it.

Again, this is to avoid upsetting or annoying people who might own a venue – not that they'd mind anyway if you were saying something nice, I'm sure, but I tend to err on the side of caution when mixing reality with fiction.

Tips from the experts

Jan Wright says:

'Life is full of great ideas. So many things we see and hear in the world have the potential to become the basis of our next plot, but reality alone is never enough. Seldom does the amusing incident we've just experienced have a gripping start or a satisfying ending so, as writers, it's our job to add those vital ingredients.

And to make stories based on reality work, I usually end up having to change several of the facts as well. It might have happened in the pub at midnight but if it's even funnier in the supermarket at lunchtime, that's where you should set it. You will not only have an improved story, but possibly your friends will still talk to you as well! Real life is great but, remember, never let facts get in the way of good fiction.'

Rachel Lovell says:

'I find I draw more and more from real life – perhaps something that happened years ago, or people or situations I have known. These events or insights form the germ of the story, but then the writer needs to use his/her imagination to create a proper plot in which (unlike real life) there is a beginning and an end.'

Chapter Fourteen

Writing Twist Endings

What is a twist-ending story?

A twist in the tale story is one which has a different, but not contrived, ending to the one expected by the reader.

The art of writing them is to conceal the clues in the text so that the reader cannot guess the ending, but when it is revealed, he or she says, "Ah, yes, of course."

In a good twist ending the reader should be able to re-read the story and find that the clues were there all along, but disguised in such a way as to make them invisible.

What works and what doesn't?

While the twist ending is of course obligatory, the story should also work in its own right, it is not a vehicle for a twist. Like any short fiction, every sentence should be relevant to the story. The plot should lead towards the twist, not be irrelevant to it.

Another common pitfall is that the writer loses sight of the market he or she is aiming the twist-ending story at. Writing twist endings for competitions offers more freedom, but if you plan to write for a magazine then your story, as well as being a twist, should fit the rest of the magazine's requirements with regard to age of character, subjects used, etc.

Types of twists

There are as many types of twist ending as there are stories, but most of them are a variation of one of the following: who? where? what? when? why?

Who?

The main character isn't who we think he or she is. For example, the character dreading his first day at college is not a nervous student, but a new tutor.

Or perhaps the characters we think are boyfriend and girlfriend are actually father and daughter.

Under the category of who twists, there are several sub-sections.

Gender twists

The main character is set up to be a woman, but is actually a man, or vice versa.

Generational twists

The characters the reader assumes are of one generation are actually another. For example, what the reader assumes are misbehaving children, are actually misbehaving parents or grandparents.

The main character is set up to be the daughter, when she is actually the mother, or vice versa.

Animal twists

The main character is set up to be a human but is actually a gerbil, cat, dog etc.

Ghost twists

The main character is set up to be alive, but is actually

dead, and vice versa.

Where?
The main character isn't where we think he is. For example, a character who is terrified of water isn't actually in the sea, but the bath.

What?
The characters are not doing what we think they are doing. For example, a character who is worn out and exhausted and appears to be in labour – is actually pushing a car that won't start, while the onlookers shout, "Push, push!"

Come-uppance twists
The door to door salesman who is intent on conning the vulnerable old lady ends up being conned by her.

Lateral thinking twists
It's possible to write a twist where the reader cannot guess the outcome – using a device such as lateral thinking. However, the twist must be logical, but be arrived at in such a way that the reader is unlikely to guess what is going on.

There are so many different types of twist that it would be impossible to list them all. All that a twist requires is to turn a situation upon its head without cheating the reader.

How to write an effective twist

Use ambiguity
Set up the reader to think that one set of events are taking place when actually something entirely different is happening by using ambiguous words.

Do engage the readers fully in the story so that they are not trying to guess what the twist might be.

Do make sure the story stands alone, i.e. it has a moment of change, a theme or universal truth, and the character has changed in some way by the end.

Do mislead readers at every opportunity, drawing them deeper into the deception.

Don't cheat. The story must stand a second read when readers check to see exactly how they were deceived.

Don't attempt overdone plot lines, unless you are sure you can bring something new to the idea.

Don't make the ending too obscure, the twist should be plain when it comes and not leave readers trying to work out whether they've missed the point, as well as the twist.

Don't make the twist so obvious you can see it coming from paragraph three!

How to check if your twist ending works

In my experience it is very difficult to know if a twist-ending story you have written works. As writers we are so close to our work that we often think our twists are too obvious – or too obscure.

The best way I know of checking if it does or doesn't work – in fact the only way I know of checking – is to test out the story on an experienced twist-ender audience.

This might be another writer or even better more than one writer, i.e. a writing class or group, either face to face or virtual. There are many forums on the internet where writers can post stories for other writers' comments.

The audience you choose must be experienced – because editors and competition judges are. Editors particularly will have seen hundreds of twist-ending stories and are skilled at guessing the outcome from paragraph one.

You will need to be skilled in the art of deception to fool them – and fool them you must if you want them to buy your story.

Tips from the experts

Marilyn Fountain says:

'If the story is to have a surprise ending, then I usually work backwards from there to a point of action at the beginning that sparks off the whole episode. I liken it to lighting the fuse that ends with the firework – and hopefully plenty of ooohs from the reader. Other stories will emerge from a particular set of circumstances, or a character or interaction between characters. I tend to 'hear' the voices and therefore the personalities and motivations of my short-story characters, rather than 'see' their physical characteristics. Sometimes it's productive to wind them up and see where they lead you. They can take you into cul-de-sacs and down blind alleys, but other times they may just take you on a wonderful journey with a satisfying destination. Very occasionally – delightfully – a more or less complete story, with characters, plot, beginning, middle and end, will pop into my head. Then it's a case of getting it down on the computer – or back of an envelope, beer mat, anything will do – before it disappears.'

Chapter Fifteen

Writing With Humour

What is humour?

I think most of us would agree that it is the quality of being funny. In fiction terms, it is a story that makes us laugh, or possibly raises a wry smile. The problem with humour is that it's such an individual thing. What makes one person laugh will make another squirm with embarrassment, or indeed may deeply offend or upset.

Of all the aspects of writing that I teach, I find humour the most divisive. I once took a class where two students very nearly came to blows over their opinions on what was funny and what was most definitely not! It is therefore one of the most difficult types of fiction to pull off.

Having said that, there is nothing more rewarding than writing humour which your audience find as funny as you – hopefully – did when you wrote it. For me, writing humour adds an extra dimension to writing. What can be better than making someone laugh?

If you do decide to write humour, you must first research your market very carefully. Your style, length and subject matter will all be determined by your intended market.

Humour for the ear

Perhaps surprisingly, short stories that are very funny when heard, for example on the radio, don't necessarily work on the page. So be aware of this. If you are writing a radio story, then it is essential to read it aloud, preferably to a group, to see if it's working. It is incredibly satisfying making people laugh – presuming that you meant your story to be funny, of course!

Humour for the eye

If you are writing humour that is aimed at a magazine or competition, then it is not a bad idea to ask someone to read your piece and see if it raises a smile. Ask more than one person. Ask them to tick the margin alongside the sections they found amusing.

Incidentally, if you are writing longer fiction which takes a period of time to read, and you are lucky enough to have a volunteer guinea pig who will read it for you, it can be extremely helpful to ask him to mark the margin in the place where he stopped reading. This may indicate that your narrative slowed or became less interesting at this point. I find this feedback device invaluable.

How to be funny without being offensive

There is a saying that it is impossible to please everyone all the time. And this is also true of readers. Nevertheless, if you are going to write humour it's helpful to try and please the majority. And of course it's essential to please your first reader, the editor or competition judge, or you won't get the chance to please anyone else. Your story will swiftly be winging its way back to you as a rejection. Once again this comes down to doing your research.

Are there any taboo subjects?

I'm not sure there are taboo subjects, as such, although of course your market will dictate this, but there are three golden rules I try not to break.

- Don't be cruel.
- Don't be crude.
- Don't be too clichéd.

If you can stick to these rules, you shouldn't go too far wrong.

What kind of humour never fails?

It is generally acceptable to make fun of yourself, but be very careful if your humour relies on poking fun at someone else. For example, husbands, or mothers-in-law, or minority groups. Situation comedy works very well if it is set up right.

Personally, I see humour on a scale. At one end there is the wry smile and at the other the rip roaring belly-laugh. This is such a matter of perception that I'm not going to give any examples, but in my experience it's easier to write the 'wry smile' type of humour because all you need is a light touch and an eye for the ridiculous.

What are the markets for humour?

The markets for humour are vast – humour is welcome across the board, but here are some suggestions you may find helpful.

Competitions
There are many competitions that ask for humorous

writing. It might be prudent to find out what type of humour the judge likes. If the judge is a well-known comedian or humorous writer, then you are well placed to aim your piece at him or her.

Magazines

Magazine editors always want humorous stories.

Before you begin, think about the age of your readers. You need to know their age because this will determine your subject matter.

As well as thinking about the reader you are trying to amuse, think about the magazine's advertisers. Magazines are justifiably concerned about offending their advertisers or readers and will not use any material, however funny, which might alienate or cause offence.

Therefore, steer clear of poking fun, however light-heartedly or even inadvertently, at a magazine's advertisers.

For example, I once wrote a light-hearted story berating cold-callers, which focused on the fact that the telephone always rings while you are in the bath. The magazine didn't publish this because they said they didn't want to upset readers who might actually have to do cold-calling themselves.

I also wrote a light-hearted story with a scene involving chickens being taken from a battery farm to their new home, but the magazine said they couldn't publish it because the chickens were transported in a car, rather than under correct humane conditions and they were worried they might get complaints from readers who were concerned about animal welfare.

These may seem extreme examples, but we are in the business of selling, so they are worth bearing in mind.

Tips from the experts

Teresa Ashby says:

'I think humour is there all the time. It's all around us. If we didn't see the funny side of situations we'd all be going round depressed and miserable. Of course there are some situations that just aren't funny, but if you're writing for laughs and find yourself smiling at what you've written, chances are your reader will smile too. I think in some ways humour is one of the most difficult things to write because if overdone it will sound forced and unreal.'

Sue Houghton says:

'Remember it isn't about you the writer showing off your own sense of humour. You have to transfer it to the character or situation and make it his or her own. Not sure you can do it? Then write your funny line, set it aside and re-read it a few days later. If it still makes you giggle, then it works.'

Chapter Sixteen

Writing With Emotion

What's the difference between emotion and sentimentality?

This is almost as difficult to answer as the question of what's funny and what isn't. It's such a personal interpretation. One reader will find a story a real tear-jerker and another reader will find exactly the same story sentimental and slushy. Perhaps more surprisingly the *same* reader might feel these two extremes about the *same* story, depending on his or her mood. But this is a factor you can't do much about. So how do you proceed?

If you're aiming for publication your first reader, as always, is your editor or competition judge. More on targeting competition judges in the next chapter. Magazines are generally easier to target. Study the stories they currently publish. They will be headed up with strap lines such as:

- One from the heart.
- A story to touch your heart.
- A touching tale.

Or other similar phrases. Read them and analyse

them and then attempt to write stories with the same level of emotion.

So how exactly do you do that? Some of the tips below may sound obvious, but they can make a lot of difference to how well a piece works.

Language
If you have a sad scene in which a character is crying, avoid overuse of the word, 'tears'.

In particular, avoid clumsy descriptions, such as, 'tears leaked from her eyes like a waterfall.' This simile I hope you'll agree is both over the top and clichéd.

It's usually better to concentrate on how your characters feel than to concentrate on the physical aspects.

For example

For a long time after she'd lost Michael, she'd felt nothing but pain. There didn't seem to be room for anything else. Some days she would realise her face was wet, though she hadn't been aware she was crying.

(I hope you'll agree this is much more effective than a simile about waterfalls!)

High stakes
For the above passage to work, your character also needs to have a strong reason for her grief. Michael would need to be her son, or her husband, for example. And the loss would need to be his death, or possibly betrayal. If he'd just left home and gone off to university, or he had gone because of some fault on her part, then the reader might not be able to empathise with her quite so much. The higher the stakes the more readers are likely to be able to empathise with the character they're reading about.

Viewpoint

Your choice of whether to use first person or third person can also make a difference. Sometimes a piece written in first person sounds more as though the character is feeling sorry for him or herself, than exactly the same piece written in third person.

The following is an extract from one of my stories, A Rose in the Gutter, published in *Take A Break*, which demonstrates this point.

A rose in the gutter – third person

> *Sarah stared out at the day with blank eyes. It was a glorious day too, from what she could see of it over her sleeping bag. The heat of summer was already in the air and, not far from where she lay, a group of students were sprawled on the grass, chatting and laughing and completely oblivious to her.*
>
> *She'd been like that once. Not a care in the world apart from her college timetable and what she would wear on her next night out. However had she come to this? Sleeping in the park with only the clothes she stood up in and the few pounds she'd managed to beg the previous day.*

The published version of A Rose in the Gutter was in third person. Now just to demonstrate a point, here is the same piece written in first person.

> *I stared out at the day with blank eyes. It was a glorious day too, from what I could see of it over my sleeping bag. The heat of summer was already in the air and, not far from where I lay, a group of students were sprawled on the grass, chatting and laughing and completely oblivious to me.*

I'd been like that once. Not a care in the world apart from my college timetable and what I would wear on my next night out. However had I come to this? Sleeping in the park with only the clothes I stood up in and the few pounds I'd managed to beg the previous day.

Because it's in first person, which tends to be more immediate, our impression of the narrator alters slightly. For a start referring to your own eyes as blank smacks a little of self pity. When the story was in third person this line was more of a visual indicator as to how the character looked.

The line *however had I come to this?* also sounds much more of a self pitying 'moan' than the line *however had she come to this?* which could almost be a line of narration.

As a reader I'd be far more inclined to want to shake the character in the second example than I'd want to shake Sarah.

And all I've altered is the viewpoint from third person to first – interesting how much difference it can make, isn't it?

How do I know if I've gone too far?

The short answer is that less is more. Emotion, rather like humour, requires a light touch.

If you are writing a story about a character who's sad, then don't dwell on the sadness for too long. Do not over-egg the pudding. Pages and pages of sadness are depressing. Move on quickly. To illustrate, here is a bit more of A Rose in the Gutter.

Not that she missed the clothes or the money – they hadn't made her happy then, and she had a feeling they wouldn't now. She missed the companionship, the banter, the feeling of belonging. She ached to feel part of the world once more. But every day she slept rough, the gap seemed to widen and the chances of her getting back seemed farther away.

No point in lying around brooding. She eased jean-clad legs out of the sleeping bag, rolled it up and put it in her back pack, and got up stiffly. A trip to the public loos to freshen up. Then maybe she'd try her luck in the subway. It was Saturday, a good day for shoppers.

Despite her dire circumstances Sarah is not going to lie around brooding and feeling sorry for herself; she is going to try and do something about her situation. Hurrah. Nobody likes a whinger! People like to see characters who are trying to make things better.

I've been using sadness as an example, but exactly the same applies to emotions at the other end of the spectrum.

If your character is happy, then great – good for her – but do not overdo happiness.

Too much focus on how wonderful everything is can swiftly become cloying and sugar-coated. It's a trap that I find is easier to fall into at the end of a story than the beginning. After all, if your character is perfectly happy at the beginning of your story and her life is absolutely wonderful, then does she really have a story to tell at all?

Here's an example of sentimental writing, which I 'achieved' simply by going over the top.

And now finally Maria held her beautiful bouncing baby in her arms and she was

141

overjoyed. Her heart swelled to bursting with maternal love. This moment for which she had waited so long was every bit as wonderful and marvellous as she'd thought it would be. She couldn't have been happier; the baby was so perfect, so beautiful, from the tips of her tiny pink toes to the gorgeous topmost hairs of her downy blonde, sweet-smelling head. Maria felt she could burst with joy. How blessed she was, how lucky, how ecstatically gloriously happy. She knew she would never complain about anything again ever.

Hmmm – I think I'd complain if I read that in a magazine – that's if I wasn't throwing up.

How about this version?

Now finally Maria held her baby in her arms and her heart swelled with love. This moment for which she had waited so long was every bit as wonderful as she'd thought it would be. Her baby was perfect, from the tips of her tiny pink toes to the top of her downy blonde head. Maria knew she would never complain about anything ever again.

I think you'll agree it's better – all I have done is remove some words to try and illustrate that less is more.

How to touch your reader – guaranteed

The only sure fire way I know of touching the reader is to write from the heart. Write honestly, hold nothing back, and keep it simple.

If you genuinely write from the heart, then your words will go to other's hearts. I have seen this in action so many times at workshops I've held. It's so important that I'm going to say it again.

What comes from the heart – goes to the heart. It really does. Try it. Get a piece of paper or sit at your computer right now. Write about something you feel passionately about. Go for it – let your emotions spill onto the page. Don't worry about going over the top in the first draft, you can edit it later.

Tips from the experts

Teresa Ashby says:

'It's no use trying to write with emotion if you don't feel it. You have to empathise with your characters, know how they must be feeling. If you have never had your home broken into, but want to write about it, you must put yourself in your character's shoes and look around your own home, imagining how gut-wrenching it would be to find it turned upside down, to see your things broken, graffiti on your walls. Imagine some stranger or strangers in your home, touching your things – it should make you shudder. You have to see situations in your mind and put yourself into them.'

Linda Mitchelmore says:

'As well as problem, people, place and plot in your story, have the whole thing hang on an emotion too – love, hate, desire, revenge, regret, hope ... and try and think of not so common ones as well ... like empathy.'

Chapter Seventeen

Writing the Competition/Literary Short Story

Writing short stories for competitions is much the same as writing them for magazines, although there are one or two subtle differences.

Let's first take a look at the similarities. You will still need a strong opening paragraph, characters that come to life, a good plot and a satisfying ending; although I feel that the endings of competitions stories can be a little different from the endings of stories aimed at some of the other markets. They are often more open-ended and the onus is on the reader to interpret what has happened.

Not that you can't do this for the magazine market too, but it tends to be more prevalent in competition stories.

What are the differences?

In my experience, one of the main differences when aiming for a competition is that you are less restricted on subject matter. This is because you aren't aiming to please a target audience with specific tastes and expectations. You are aiming to please a judge.

You may of course target the judge, but this is

generally more difficult, although doing some research may help. Your judge is probably a writer, so does he or she write humour, thrillers, crime, romance or something completely different? Bear in mind judges may well find stories that aren't in their own genres more appealing – so knowing what they write is not necessarily an accurate guide.

If they say what they are looking for, then pay attention. Some competitions have a reputation for preferring the literary short story. And in my opinion this is the other crucial difference when writing the competition story.

What is a literary short story?

This is a question I'm often asked and I'm not sure there is a definitive answer.

My interpretation is that the term literary usually refers to good use of language. So a literary short story as opposed to a commercial short story (and it's perfectly possible to have both) is one where the use of language is very important – perhaps more important than the plot.

There tends to be more scope for simile and metaphor. Literary writing is often poetic and usually beautiful to read. The reader has time to linger over a wonderful phrase or passage. Clichés are definitely out and imagery is paramount. The writing has rhythm and may be referred to as lyrical.

This doesn't mean you can dispense with the plot and get carried away with long passages of beautiful description. Most of us, myself included, are in love with words. We probably wouldn't be writers if we weren't, but make sure your story still works.

I was told, when I first started writing commercially that my writing was too literary for magazines – this might sound hard to believe, these days, when I write for magazines so much, but it was true then. There is a part of me that mourns for some of those beautiful phrases. In fact, I'll let you into a secret, although I cut out many more literary phrases than ever go into my short stories, I do my best to slip the odd one in. Beautiful phrases incidentally sit very well amongst several plainer ones. Rather like the fact that one daisy on a lawn can be very attractive, whereas dozens of daisies might be a little too much.

Anyway, back to literary writing. My writing tutor, Ian Burton, is a master of the literary short story. His use of language is beautiful and so I will use an example of one of his short stories to illustrate what to my mind is literary writing.

This is the opening of Six Windows High, by Ian Burton:

The cats were settled on the grassy centre of The Close – perfectly polite distances between them – but their silences were not far short of being angry.

As leader, Marvin knew it was for him to break the silence but he was too angry with Gandalf to do so. This old-versus-young rivalry, this Marvin versus Gandalf thing, was getting out of reach. And it would soon force the other cats into taking sides. It was as if the anger between them was being bounced on the end of a string – and they both had to pounce – no matter what.

At last, Marvin, treading softly on the silence,

*said, "I don't think any of us should take any
undue risks trying to get a closer look at this
"Princess-cat" – as Gandalf calls her. That's
my advice. She's only ever been seen in the
window at the top of the Tower Block. No cat
has reported either scent or sight of her down
here."*

Gandalf, the central character, has fallen in love with a
cat who is trapped in a tower block and against the
advice of the older and wiser cats, wants to rescue her.
It is the way the story is written that makes it so
delightful. Here are some phrases I've picked out from
further in to the story.

Gandalf's eyes opened. It was time.
*He knew with his first tread, his first touch of
the carpet, that this was his dusk and his dusk
alone and he stepped into the grain of the air
without disturbing it or ruffling his whiskers.*

What a beautiful way of saying he's on his way to
rescue the captured princess. It's not just lovely writing,
it's very evocative of cats. And it will be no surprise to
learn that Ian loves cats.

*He waited. The first chance came along but he
judged it safer to let her go by: a tall She-human
with clickety-clicky paws and so thin she cast
little or no shadow.*
*Gandalf knew who he was waiting for – a soft
treading woman who cast a wonderful summer
shadow. He'd flirted with her once or twice – in
the summer-time, when she and her shadow
were out walking.*

Again, this is wonderful imagery as Gandalf waits for

his chance to enter the tower block. We accompany Gandalf on his rescue mission and he manages to slip in the main entrance with a human going in the same direction. There is a lovely description of a lift:

He watched astonished as the shiny doorway at the other end of the passage suddenly slitted apart and the air and the noise coughed out a human, before closing again.

Gandalf is now on the right floor of the tower block, but where does he go from here?

All these doors and he didn't know which one – he'd thought his nose would tell him. And how hard was it going to be to get out again, accompanied, he hoped, by the Princess – but a Princess who probably wasn't hunting fit, having been trapped in a tower with nothing but bits of string to chase...

He set about the immediate task which was to calm his thoughts. With his ears focused behind him – and his eyes and nose focused ahead – he settled on the cold and drafty top step.

First things first – which door was the Princess's? Only his nose could tell him this. Only patient concentration could enable decision. A watchful, sensitised calm took over. With immense concentration it became possible to separate each aroma coming from beneath each of the doors. He worked through them all fixing a direction onto each. Finally, he reached the faintest of faint smells, from a cat – from the Princess. It was coming from the door on his left at the far end of the passage, closest to the shiny doors.

His senses relaxed a little. Now purpose had a direction.

The next whoosh coughed out an elderly woman. She moved with easy-peasy slowness towards the door Gandalf wanted opened. Eventually, after much jangling, she opened it. Once inside – the faint cat smell both reassured and disturbed him.

Once inside, he doubled back on his tracks to get into the shadow of the woman. But his alert brilliance was wasted. The woman was so slow he had time to sit and wait for her to pass by.

The woman went off to the kitchen but Gandalf slid into an unlit room, following the still faint scent.

And he saw the Princess. She was sitting at the window – just as he knew she would be – looking for him probably. The first of moon's light was playing in her fur, streaking through its silver, diving into and out of its black.

He found cover at the side of the sofa, proud that he could do so without distracting her but also miffed that her nose seemed not to detect his presence. Admiration and awe at her perfect stillness tempered the hurt of this insult.

But then the light went on and the woman came with her cold food on a plate. Sounds of a kettle-on streamed in from the kitchen.

The woman sat on the sofa and began to eat.

The Princess did not turn to look, did not greet the woman in any way – not even with a flick of her ear. Nor was there any response when the woman started speaking. Nothing and no one in the room responded to her – except Gandalf.

Gandalf, eyes only for the Princess, could only hear what Monroe had said about the Princess being a stuff-toy... He'd never seen a cat so beautiful and so real. And this stillness of hers was... awesome.

The woman stopped eating. She got up and went to the Princess and removed her from the window. Gandalf knew there was something wrong with the Princess.

The momentary wand of the Princess's fixed gaze seared Gandalf as she was taken back to the sofa. The woman cuddled her and speech-purred deeply. And her call affected Gandalf just as deeply – but there was something, badly horrifyingly wrong here.

The horrifying truth is in fact that Gandalf's princess isn't alive. She has died and been stuffed by her elderly owner.

He couldn't place any of this anywhere in his experience. Next thing he knew, the woman had him in her eyes. The Princess was stiff under the woman's arm but she too had him fixed in her still, still eyes. And all three were held on the moment of their next-move intentions. From the woman's arms Princess spoke and the distant message melted into meaning from the chill of her eyes: 'I come from far away. This human is kind. She loved me. I knew freedom. I knew love of others. I knew much love of me. I sleep the dream of the slept very well.''

Even though the princess tells him this truth, Gandalf is reluctant to believe it. He just knows he has to escape from the nightmare that his rescue mission has become.

The resolution of this story is that Gandalf never really believes what he has seen with his own eyes. He is not prepared to accept the older cat's wisdom – he would rather let go of reality than give up on his dreams. It is a poignant resolution to a powerful story. And like every good story it contains a powerful universal truth. Sometimes reality is too hard to face, so we hold on to our own perception of this.

Yes, this is a story about cats, but the wisdom of it could just as easily be applied to humans. And of course the story will be read by humans not cats.

This story was a quarterly winner in the Worldwide Writers competition and was published in their 1999 anthology.

This brings me on to another point about competitions. The scope is often far wider than that of other markets. Using animal viewpoints tends to be a taboo amongst magazines.

What about competitions that aren't billed as literary?

There are many of these. Some are run by writing magazines or small presses, some are internet competitions, some are annual competitions that produce an anthology. If you can, look at previous winners. If the same judge is used each year, you can get a good idea of what the organisers are looking for. You can then target them in much the same way as you'd do for any other market.

What can I do to improve my chances in a competition?

It may sound simple, but study the rules. I've heard

many a judge bemoaning the fact that they've had to discard/disqualify a well-written story because the writer did not stick to the rules.

Word limits

If there is a word limit, stick to it. If they state a maximum of 1000 words, then they don't want a story of 1002 words. If you are disqualified then you will have wasted your entry fee, not to mention the hard work of writing the story in the first place.

Themes

If a theme or subject is specified, steer clear of the obvious interpretation. If it's obvious to you; then it will probably be obvious to every other entrant, too.

Deadlines

It goes without saying that you must not miss the deadline. If the rules state that your story must be in by 4.00 pm on a particular date – and many do – then make sure yours arrives in time.

But another common mistake writers make is to write their story at the last minute and not leave enough time for editing. Even experienced writers make this mistake. It is far better to allow an extra week or two and leave time for your story to cool on the page, and then have a thorough edit before you send it off.

Tips from the experts

Ian Burton says:

'When I'm judging a short-story competition, one of the qualities I look for is the memorability factor. I read all the entries at one sitting, and then over the next few days I'll find that one or two of them will rise to the surface of my mind. It is very often these memorable stories that make it to the top of the pile. So my advice to a writer entering competitions would be to make your story as different as possible. Steer clear of familiar themes.'

Sandy Neville says:

'The Richard & Judy Children's Story Competition attracted 10,000 entries. To say I was stunned to be one of 25 finalists would be an understatement. I still think back to the thrill of appearing on live television and seeing my story in print and on the shelves of a major bookstore. That one event convinced me that I actually could write and has spurred me on to try and achieve publication in my own right. I know one day I will succeed.'

Jean Saunders says:

'Writing for short-story competitions means obeying the basic rules that each entry requires. Always read them carefully. The rules may vary according to each competition, but in general they will be simple to follow, and each one is important if you want your entry to be considered. Failure to stick to any competition rules means you risk being disqualified, and all your hard work will have been for nothing.

• You will usually be required to write your story to a certain number of words. Don't try to impress the judges by varying this number of words to suit your story. In particular, don't overshoot the wordage.

• You are often given a set subject or genre to write about, which may be one that you have not thought about writing before. Use your imagination to come up with something different from all the other entries. Think laterally to give yourself every chance of succeeding.

• You may be asked to provide a pseudonym, not only to give all entrants a fair chance, but also to avoid favouritism with judges who may know your name. Keep it simple and not ridiculous.

• You must submit your story before a certain date. Don't miss it by leaving your entry until the last moment. Give yourself plenty of time to write your story and to do any revisions.

• You will usually have to pay an entry fee. Don't forget to include it with your story. Fill in any forms that are required and don't add anything more about yourself!'

Chapter Eighteen

Writing Ghost Stories

Ghost stories always have been – and I suspect always will be – popular with magazines and competitions alike.

Are there rules for writing ghost stories?

However, odd as it may seem, there are certain rules when writing about ghosts. These have been relaxed a little over the years in the sense that ghosts can now do far more than they used to be able to! They're no longer confined to yelling, "woo woo woo," and clanking the odd chain, although they may still do that if you wish. Ghosts, like everything else in life, have evolved and become more sophisticated.

I think the main rule is consistency, – if your ghost cannot be touched by a living creature, if it's possible to actually walk through your ghost – then it should also not be possible for your ghost to 'pick up' solid objects. A ghost cannot, for example, pick up a cat and have it on its lap! Although, they can feasibly still move solid objects around – I think they can do the latter via the power of their minds, as poltergeists do!

Do ghosts have minds? Well, I guess they must

have, seeing as they don't have any bodies. They have to have something, poor souls – pun intended! Complicated, isn't it?

The modern ghost, and very possibly the more traditional type, can also talk, make noises, create smells, materialise and de-materialise at will, and do all the things they used to do like walk through walls and create cold atmospheres.

I think in certain circumstances they can probably also touch humans. But I don't think ghosts should be able to eat, unless they're eating ghostly food – that would be fine. I'd personally have trouble believing in a ghost who could eat solid food and then disappear through the wall of a house five minutes later. For me, this would be a contradiction.

It's probably easier if you establish early on exactly what your particular ghost can and cannot do, and stick to the rules. If you want it to touch living things, then living things should probably also be able to touch it.

Because – strange as it may seen – although we're asking readers to suspend belief, we still need them to be able to believe in the world we've created. The last thing we want is for the reader – or the editor – to be shouting, "For goodness' sake, that's ridiculous!" at our manuscripts.

This also applies to science fiction or fantasy writing. What is and isn't possible should be clearly established from the beginning if you want your reader to stay with you.

Try something different

Ghost stories are very popular, which means it's hard to find a new and original approach. If you're trying to sell, you will need to think laterally. In the traditional ghost story the restless spirit often haunts a place such as an old house or a castle. How about a ghost that haunts a motorway services café or a ghost that haunts a field or even a tree? Alternatively, you might like to write about a ghost that doesn't stay in one place, but moves around. Perhaps it haunts a family or individual.

Ghosts and exorcisms go together, but think laterally here too. One of the best ghost stories I ever read was about a woman who'd exorcised an annoying ghost and then missed him and tried to get him back again.

Try a humorous ghost story, or a romantic ghost story. Or how about an animal ghost?

Rational explanations

Some markets will specify that they'd like the suggestion of a more down to earth explanation for the ghost: i.e. was it a ghost or was there really a rational explanation for the strange goings on? You could leave it open-ended so the reader can decide.

Tips from the experts

Kath McGurl says:

'Write at night. Dim the lights in your writing room, but leave the curtains open, so that anyone or any*thing* could be looking in at you. Write late, when everyone else has gone to bed. Write after a glass or two of wine, to free your imagination. Write scared.'

Mhari Grant says:

'For me a spine-tingling story can arise from the human psyche. Most people live within certain moral perimeters but what if a character, while appearing normal, had a skewed view of the world? Uncertainty together with a frisson of danger and fear can be invoked by this scenario. A one-night stand that wouldn't go away or a stalker falls into this category. Stalking was the premise of one of my stories but with a twist. The character thought that he was being stalked by his mad and dead girlfriend who had committed suicide. He was vulnerable and on the edge when one night he pushes his tormentor down a dark, unlit stairway. Only to find that the lifeless form at the bottom of the stairs wasn't his dead girlfriend but an innocent neighbour

If there is a supernatural element to the story I like it to arise out of the everyday and ordinary and for the ghost to serve a purpose other than to scare. For example in one story I had a woman alone in the office at night trying to get to grips with some new software on her computer. A colleague, whom she'd stood up for earlier against their draconian boss, comes back and helps her, restoring her confidence and self-esteem. She is buzzing with excitement until a phone call informs her that he was killed in a car accident on the way home from work.'

Chapter Nineteen

Writing Crime Stories

If you're a fan of crime stories, then the good news is that there are lots of markets where you can place your work.

What types of crime story are there?

There are as many types of crime story as there are crimes, but here are some of the most saleable types.

Whodunit?
They often start with an unexplained murder or theft and the writer's job is to keep the reader guessing until the end. They might involve a detective or an amateur sleuth. Both work well.

Cosy crime
There are probably lots of definitions of a cosy crime story but my definition is a story which is written in a fairly light-hearted manner. The writer will need a light touch and the crime won't be too heinous or if it is, it might happen offstage. The object of a cosy crime story is to entertain the reader, not scare her witless. Think Midsomer Murders.

Crime twists

These are as many and varied as any other kind of twists. Here are a few examples:

- You think the character is committing a crime, but he is actually doing something perfectly legal.
- The perpetrator of the crime is not what he or she seems.
- The victim of the crime is not what he or she seems.
- Victim and perpetrator are actually reversed at the end of the story.

How do I construct a crime story?

Well, this is up to you, but the first thing you'll need to think about is probably the crime, followed closely by the character's motivation for committing it. You don't necessarily have to reveal the character's motivation, particularly if it's part of your twist, but you should know it.

Your crime might range from a character cheating to win a competition to your character committing a murder. The crime doesn't have to be major.

If your story is a whodunit then you will also at some stage have to reveal to the reader who did do it, perhaps at the end as a twist. Or the twist could be why the perpetrator did it.

I find that writing crime stories is a little like doing a jigsaw in that you have several strands of the storyline with different pieces of information that don't come together or complete the picture until the end. I once wrote a serial for *Woman's Weekly* where the main character was being terrorised by anonymous notes. When I began the serial I didn't know who was sending the notes – or why – but as the story progressed I introduced the reader to a series of characters who could have been sending them. Each of them had a different motivation and at the end I had to choose which one it would be.

I don't plot particularly – I like to let the drama unfold naturally – and I like to let the characters lead me. Some writers plot meticulously. The only way to find out which method works for you is to practise.

What are the markets for crime?

There are often competitions asking for crime stories. Check the internet for up to date competitions – it helps to put a date range in as many older competitions will still come up on search engines.

As I've already mentioned there are several slots for crime in women's magazines too.

Are there any taboos?

Yes, I think there are and they're all related to your market, so do check their requirements carefully. But here are some general tips.

- Try to avoid overused themes.
- Don't be too graphic or bloodthirsty. Your reader might be happy to read about how a murder is solved, but he or she won't necessarily want the details of blood dripping through floorboards or the victim's tongue turning blue as the killer tightens the noose around his neck!

There is a golden rule with most types of fiction, and crime is no exception. You are in the entertainments industry. So entertain.

Tips from the experts

Adrian Magson says:

'I write crime stories for magazines, although I tend to use my own name as it allows me a bit of exposure for my novels. And there's a link there, because my main character in my novels, which is a series, is a young woman – a reporter. I think this came about after writing about women for so many years (OK, and knowing that women form the biggest crime novel readership, too).'

Chapter Twenty

Writing Erotic Short Stories

This book wouldn't be complete without a chapter on writing erotic short stories. I have published a few of these and I also run an erotic writing workshop, which comes with a light-hearted warning that students should bring with them an open mind. I also mention that my course is possibly not suitable for writers with a sensitive disposition.

So maybe I should write a similar warning to readers of this chapter. If you are not interested in writing erotica, please skip this chapter. However, there is a growing market for erotic short stories, and while many of the rules are the same as for writing any other short story, there are one or two differences. I'll try to cover them here.

What's the difference between an erotic short story and an ordinary one?

In my opinion, the main difference is that the erotic short story will have a love scene, sex scene, call it what you will and your reader will want to go beyond the bedroom door. Here are some tips that I've found helpful with the writing of such scenes.

Choose your settings carefully
You may want your characters to be adventurous, but it is usually wise to choose a setting which is private. A deserted moonlit cove might be acceptable, whereas a crowded beach is probably not!

Be careful about logistics
When you are writing a love scene it is vital to check that what you're describing is physically possible and not too uncomfortable! Logistics are very important in erotic fiction or your reader may well think, 'yeah right, that's impossible' and give up reading.

Don't be unrealistic
By the same token, your love scene will be more believable if it has some basis in reality. In reality, sex is not necessarily instant orgasms, bells ringing and pinnacles of ecstasy. Fiction should echo reality, at least to some degree!

Be realistic, but don't be crude. Incidentally, humour can work very well.

How important are the senses?

They're always important, but in erotic writing, they're critical. Describe sensations: taste; smell; touch and above all emotion. Done with great sensitivity, this is what will make your erotic stories work.

What about plot and storyline?

Make sure your story stands alone and isn't just a vehicle for a sex scene. This is more important for some markets than for others. In fact for some markets, the opposite might apply. Do your market research.

Are there any taboos?

This might seem a strange question when the very subject can be taboo, but yes there often are. Check the editorial guidelines for your intended market. Most have them. Most exclude sex acts involving children/bestiality/rape or violence. Do check that your submission fits the criteria.

Is writing erotica more difficult?

Personally, I think that it is, although I didn't think that before I tried it. The following are some tips for you to get in the mood – these are tips for you, not your characters, who hopefully are already in the mood!

Relax
Set the scene. Light a scented candle on your desk and pour a glass of your favourite tipple.

Leave your inhibitions behind
On no account should you be worrying about what your partner/mother/sister will think when he or she reads your sex scene because this will almost certainly inhibit you.

Remember that people reading your sex scene will not automatically assume you have experienced whatever it is you are describing. Well, they might, but they'd be wrong, wouldn't they? After all, if you were writing a murder scene from the killer's point of view, you'd be using your imagination. Point this out to any Smart Alecs who might try to embarrass you!

What sort of language should I use?

Use language that you feel comfortable with. But more importantly, make sure that it also reflects your characters' viewpoints.

Are your characters 'making love' or 'bonking'? How would they refer to each other's bodies? Does she have 'great boobs' or 'a magnificent bosom'? Does he have a 'cute behind' or 'the best bum she'd ever set eyes on'?

Chances are you will be writing about characters you care about – but they might not be that similar to you. So bear this in mind.

Choose the viewpoint your sex scene will be written in. A female character will probably describe the event differently from a male character and I'm talking emotionally here, not physically. Emotions and senses are key when writing erotic fiction.

Euphemisms
Steer clear of euphemisms. Do not describe your hero slipping his 'throbbing manhood' into the heroine's 'tunnel of love'. Your reader is more likely to fall about laughing than be aroused.

Correct words
Use the correct anatomical words sparingly or you might find your prose reads like a text book.

So if you can't use euphemisms and you can't use 'correct' words, where does this leave you?

Some 'correct' words are more acceptable than others. For example it's generally fine to use words like nipples, buttocks and breasts. Bear in mind there are many erogenous zones on the body, for example, the curve of a back or hip or even a bare shoulder. Be sensitive.

Suggestion is sometimes enough
For example, *he lowered himself on to her and with uncertain fingers guided himself inside her.*

Presuming there has been sufficient build up, there is no doubt about what he is doing, is there? It is not necessary (again depending on the market) to be too specific.

Should I mention contraception?

Again, your market may well provide guidelines. But generally, if your characters are making love for the first time, and/or don't know each other very well, then you will need to consider this. You don't necessarily need to dwell on it, but it's worth giving it a passing mention. Even if it's in a character's thoughts. In today's world it would be unrealistic and slightly irresponsible (as in real life) to disregard contraception altogether!

Timing

This is very important. I'm not talking about what time your characters engage in sexual relations, but at what point in the story they do it. It will depend – obviously – on your plot line. But generally speaking sex starts long before the bedroom (again as in real life). The moment at which your characters 'get it together' should be climactic. No pun intended. Readers should know they've been building towards this point and be wanting it to happen.

During this build up you will have achieved some sexual tension between your characters.

Length

I'm talking number of words here! This depends entirely on you. Some writers can go on for pages and pages. Personally, I find that a little tedious both to write and to read. But this is very personal. There are two factors to consider. The main one is market. The other is what you feel comfortable with.

Health warning

When you are writing your sex scene do not be surprised if you feel aroused yourself. This is a good sign. The more you are able to get inside your characters' heads the better your writing will be – whatever you're writing about.

NB: If you have a partner it might be as well to warn them!

Should I use a pseudonym?

This is one of the most common questions I'm asked. My view on this is that if you are published in other markets and are at all worried that readers of these markets might be shocked or offended by seeing your name on erotic fiction, then you should use a pseudonym. Some writers would say that this applies to any type of writing you do which is substantially different from your core markets.

How important is market research?

You probably already know what I'm going to say here. Market research is always the most important ingredient when you are writing to sell – but in an erotic market it is absolutely critical. Study your intended market carefully. How explicit you can or should be, will be dictated by what the publisher wants.

What markets are there?

Magazines

There are obviously the top-shelf magazines, some of which carry fiction. Some are aimed at men and some at women and there's a huge difference in what their readers feel happy to read. Research is the key to finding out what the editor will and won't publish.

Mainstream magazines rarely carry erotic stories, although, in some, you may be able to allude to your characters making love.

Competitions
There are an awful lot of erotica competitions and you will need to study the rules and guidelines provided to see how explicit these stories should be.

Short story anthologies
Again, you will need to study the guidelines carefully and if possible look at previously published anthologies in the series. Any publisher who requests erotic fiction for anthologies, for example, Accent Press, will also provide guidelines on request.

The internet
There are opportunities here, too, but a word of warning. If you type erotica into a search engine you may be diverted to – how do I put this? – all sorts of "interesting" websites. My advice would be to make sure you include the word writing.

Tips from the experts

David Wass writes erotic stories for Scarlet. He says:

'My dictionary defines 'erotica' as *explicit sexual literature or art*, and 'explicit' as *leaving little to the imagination.* How much allowance is given to the imagination is up to the author. To me, if it's a lot then it's romance; if there's none it's pornography. Personally I like to leave little.'

Cathryn Cooper is the author of five erotic novels, plus several short stories. She also edited the first nine titles for Xcite Books, published by Accent Press. She says:

'First and foremost, there must be a STORY. I've heard people comment that writing an erotic story is easy; all you have to do is write dirty. Sorry. It doesn't work. Story still counts. The main character must have some motivation for what is happening. A sequence of sexual scenarios without character, pace or point is about as exciting as last week's shopping list.'

Ron Edwards writes magazine short stories and erotic stories for anthologies. He says:

'Two basic ingredients that for me make a good erotic story: first, plenty of humour – if you consider the extraordinary lengths that humans go to in pursuit of 'it' then it has to be funny; secondly, the storyline. I write the sort of stories that work just as well if you take out the erotic. I sold one story three times – first erotic – second as a straight story – and lastly as one that was just a little bit suggestive.'

Chapter Twenty-one

Men Writing for Women's Magazines

Writing short stories is a joy (and a struggle) whoever you are, and all of the advice in this book is about how to do it, not who you are. But I am often asked questions by men who want to write for women's magazines – so here are some of them.

What are the best short-story markets for men?

I think this goes back to what you enjoy reading. I've mentioned before that it's easier to write stories you like reading than to force yourself to write stories you wouldn't read, so keep this in mind. If you love horror or sci-fi or crime then find a market that publishes it and go from there.

Can men successfully write for women's magazines?

The answer to this is a resounding yes. There are lots of men writing very successfully for women's magazines, my stepson, Adam Millward, being one of them. Adam sold his first short story to *Woman's Weekly* when he was fourteen. It was a story about a young boy in hospital.

He then went on to sell dozens of stories in both

male and female viewpoint to women's magazines. I occasionally hear it said that Adam had a huge advantage on the writing front being related to me (heaven forbid!) and he is the first to admit that he was pleased I could point him in the right direction. But just to set the record straight he sent out his first few dozen stories to magazines under a pseudonym and from a different address, specifically so he wouldn't be linked to me. I was worried that if he did sell to a magazine someone might one day say to him – that my influence (what influence?) – could have helped him.

So when he did sell – and he sent out fifteen or so stories before he had an acceptance – he knew he'd done it on his own merit and not because we share a name.

If anyone else out there has a family member who is following in his or her writing footsteps, and is struggling with the same dilemma, then we can strongly recommend our course of action.

Will I need a female pseudonym?

It's entirely up to you. Some men prefer to write under a pseudonym, some don't. It certainly won't affect editors' decisions. Why should it? First and foremost they are looking for stories that suit their readership. The gender of the author is irrelevant.

If you do want to conceal your gender, regardless of whether you are male or female, then you might want to consider using your initial rather than using your full name.

Adam abandoned his female pseudonym once he was established and now writes as A Millward.

Aren't women's magazines all knitting and romance?

Not these days. In fact they haven't been for a long time, although there still seems to be a widely held belief that women's fiction has to be romantic. Pop into your local newsagent and have a look at some of the magazines carrying fiction. Short stories have never been so varied. Some magazines welcome crime, sci-fi and ghost stories and the twist-ending story is eternally popular.

What are the markets other than women's magazines?

Other markets include: radio; small presses; competitions; erotica and anthologies. Some newspapers also carry fiction, which because it is aimed at a readership that is both male and female, can be a very good place to start.

Tips from the experts

Adrian Magson says:

'I started from the simplest standpoint – that of wanting to write. Without that, I'd never have got anywhere. I began writing for women's magazines purely because there wasn't much market for the stuff I liked, which was crime/thriller material. So I did what everyone always advises, I studied the market, decided I could do that... and after the usual mountain of rejection slips (!) managed to start selling here and there.

As for writing for the women's market, I knew what my mother liked to read, which was my main benchmark. I also knew the kind of things I was capable of writing, and *by keeping to the magazines' guidelines* (always important), it seemed to pay off. I think what helped was that I avoided going too deep into a woman's psyche in my stories (difficult material to write about with any ease for a man, anyway) and used humour a lot, so that's probably how I managed it. I also didn't – and don't – push the envelope too much (if XYZ is what a magazine wants – that's what I write).

I also didn't get precious about my writing. You want the ending changed? Sure. You don't like the names? No problem. And as for my fantastically inventive titles... I can't offhand recall a single magazine ever using one!

As for using a female pen-name, I was asked by a magazine (*My Weekly*) to write pieces for a regular humorous column (A Lighter Look at Life), but I thought it looked odd writing from a female perspective with a man's name at the top. So we agreed to me using Ellen Cleary, and I wrote dozens of pieces for them under that name (what Ann describes as me putting on my mental frock). This later spread into being used for first person female stories – so a big nod to me mum for that! Again, it was what suited the magazine, not an attempt to deceive readers – and in any case, the LL pieces were all taken from real events, bar none.'

Adam Millward says:

'I don't really have any 'tricks' for getting into the mind of the woman (I haven't tried seeking inspiration wearing a skirt or a pair of high heels to date!) It's sometimes easy to assume that men and women see everything from a diametrically opposed perspective, but in my opinion it all comes down to creating a human character who will effectively carry the plot, regardless of gender. Anything more specific (like understanding how it feels to be pregnant) can only be overcome by the writer's age-old necessity – research. I've found relatives and friends (male or female) are only too happy to share an experience from their own point of view.'

Chapter Twenty-two

Working With Editors

Is it necessary to write covering letters?

I'm often asked if it's necessary to write covering letters when submitting by post. I think this is a decision best left to individual writers. Personally, I very rarely send a covering letter with my fiction. Where is the need when everything you want to tell the fiction editor: i.e. the title of the story, your name, address and the number of words is already on your cover sheet?

A good reason to write a covering letter

However, there is the question of building a relationship with editors and I would recommend sending a brief covering letter in certain circumstances. If a fiction editor has been kind enough to send you comments on an individual story, perhaps asking you to rewrite it with some changes, then it's polite to send a covering letter back with your rewritten submission, which might go something like this:

Dear fiction editor (insert name)

Thank you so much for taking the trouble to

comment on the attached story. I have rewritten it to include the changes you suggest and will look forward to hearing if it is closer to publication standard.

   Thanks once again for your help.
   Yours sincerely
   (your name)

Another good reason to write a covering letter

I'd also recommend that you send a covering letter with your next story if the editor has recently bought a story from you for the first time. This is to ensure your next story goes straight to that individual and doesn't end up on the slush pile.

You might also want to enclose a covering letter if you've had some publishing success and want to tell a new market about your previous experience.

Do check the guidelines of the market to which you're submitting or the rules of the competition. They might actually tell you whether a letter is required or not. I must stress that I'm only talking about short-story submissions. If you're submitting non-fiction or novels, you will need a covering letter.

Although I rarely send letters I do almost always send a compliment slip – this is more to be polite than for any other reason, although it is handy to mention that this story is part of a series, or is a response to a previous request, for example, for summer stories.

Can I submit by email?

Again, you'll need to check the submission guidelines for your market, or the competition rules. Never just assume you can send unsolicited manuscripts via email. If you are submitting by email, you'll need to check whether your market requires attachments or the work to be pasted into the body of the email.

How to present your work

This is not as simple as it once was, as some markets now state exactly how they'd like work to be presented, down to whether to use single or double quotation marks for dialogue. If your market does this, then follow their guidelines exactly. Otherwise, the following rules are generally fine:

The practicalities

- Use reasonable quality white A4 paper and type in double line spacing on one side of the paper only.
- Use an easy to read font. I use Times New Roman, font size 13.
- Left and right hand margins should be approximately 1 inch.
- The first sheet should be the title page. This should include your name and address, (phone number and email address optional) the title of the story and the approximate number of words. It should also include the letters F.B.S.R.O. (First British Serial Rights offered)
- On page one of the manuscript you should repeat your name and address and the title of the story.
- The title and page number should also appear on each page of the manuscript.
- Do not staple the manuscript, unless asked, a paper clip is fine. Do not bind the manuscript either and most importantly, do not put it in a plastic sheet.

There's a very practical reason for this latter point. Ever noticed how slippery those plastic sheets are? Imagine an editor with a desk full of those, she'd spend more time retrieving them from the floor than reading them!

Some less obvious, but still important points
If you smoke, then don't do it while printing manuscripts. In fact it is best to keep your paper away from smoke altogether. Smoke has a habit of clinging to paper and the last response you want from your editor or judge is to have her wrinkle her nose before she's read so much as your opening paragraph.

Make sure your manuscript is as perfect as possible. Chances are there will be mistakes you haven't noticed – however many times you've read your work. So make sure there aren't mistakes you have noticed.

Return postage
You should always include an SAE so that your story or acceptance letter can be returned to you.

I submit anything up to 6 pages in an A5 envelope, folded once, with an accompanying A5 envelope for its return. Over 6 pages I'd use an A4 envelope.

If a story is rejected and it looks as though it hasn't been read – I would still reprint it before sending it out again. You can tell by the level of 'crease' in a manuscript that it has been out before, and if I was an editor deciding what to buy, I might observe that another editor has turned this down, so why should I want it?

Timing
Expect to wait two to three months for a reply. Some markets are much quicker than this, some much slower.

How soon can I chase up a manuscript?

This is a difficult one – in my experience if you chase up a manuscript, most editors will send it back to you, even if they were considering buying it. So you might be inviting a rejection.

For this reason I'd wait at least six months. I've often waited longer than this. I've sold short stories that have been out up to a year after submission.

If you have been waiting a very long time – seven or eight months, then you could always resubmit, enclosing a covering letter saying you think the manuscript may have gone astray in the post and are therefore resubmitting. This can sometimes prompt a positive response.

Keeping track of your stories

It is vital to keep track of where your stories are. You might think you'll remember, but you won't – trust me.

I keep paper records – although you might prefer to have electronic ones. It's a quirk of mine – I spend so much time at my PC that I like to have a break between stories and fill in a paper record – I find it more satisfying. I keep three lots of records.

1) A card index box. Each story has its own card and they're filed in alphabetical order. The story title and number of words is at the top of the card. Beneath that, I write a list of markets to where I'm intending to send the story, plus the date of submission and return and any comments the editor might make. If more than one editor makes the same comment, for example, this is contrived, or predictable, then I'll rewrite the story. I might do it on one such comment unless I feel strongly otherwise.

2) I keep an A4 sheet, headed up with my markets, see example. (This shows, at a glance, how many stories are out where and how long they've been there.) When

a story is sold or rejected I cross it out. When the sheet is full I use a new one.

Woman's weekly	My weekly	Take a Break	People's friend	Others
title and date	title and date	title and date	title and date	Title, date and market

3) I also keep a monthly sheet with my work completed on it, see example. I find that seeing exactly what work I've done motivates me. It's all too easy to let weeks slip by with nothing actually having been sent out.

Week	Type	Title	Words	Market	Paid
1	New				
	Submitted				
	Others				
2	New				
	Submitted				
	Others				
3	New				
	Submitted				
	Others				
	Totals				

4) I've just realised there's actually a fourth set of records. I list all the stories I write on a separate sheet with dates, just so I can keep an annual tally. It's quite good fun filling in the market achieved section and means I can keep an accurate record of the percentage sold. It also means I can analyse which markets I sell the most to in any given month or year.

Month	Title	Market	Type	Fee	Date paid	Total earned
Jan						
Feb						
Mar						
Apr						
May						
Jun						
Jul						
Aug						
Sep						
Oct						
Nov						
Dec						

As you can see I like my records! But the only strictly necessary one is to keep a note of where your work is, when it was sent and when it was returned or bought.

Working with editors overseas

Email submissions make it far easier to submit stories to overseas markets. Some overseas markets are listed in *The Writer's Handbook.*

Research is more difficult if you don't have copies of the magazines, but you can submit to English-speaking countries quite easily. The internet is a handy research tool.

Tips from the experts

Liz Smith, fiction editor of *My Weekly*, has this to say:

'Be it fantasy, sci fi, supernatural, or traditional, my ideal story introduces you to characters you want to know better, in places you may never have visited but can visualise perfectly. It should take you on a journey of surprises where the final destination though impossible to predict is more than you could have hoped for.'

Jennie Bohnet says:

'Targeting the right market for your stories is crucial and if an editor takes the time to give some feedback on a rejection – read and inwardly digest, editors know what they are talking about. Lots of markets are accepting e-mail submissions these days so it is very easy to write a story and dash it off – no searching for stamps and catching the last post, just a press of a button and your story is winging its way to fame and fortune. Before you press that button, print the story out – mistakes are picked up much more easily on the printed page than on screen and, a final tip, make sure the message in your e-mail is grammatically right, with correct spelling and punctuation – remember this is the first bit of your writing that an editor is going to read and you don't want to get off on the wrong foot.'

Chapter Twenty-three

Tax and Record Keeping

Must I pay tax on my writing income?

The short answer is yes – if you are already using your tax allowance in a job other than writing.

If you are writing to sell – and you wouldn't be reading this book if you weren't, then there will come a time when you will need to pay tax. I strongly advise that you keep detailed records of income and expenditure, including receipts and invoices from the moment you begin.

It is possible to claim past expenditure against future earnings. Talk to an accountant for more information.

Like many writers, I had a full-time job for many years, and wrote in my spare time. I employed an accountant from the beginning – accountant's fees are tax deductible – and I wanted to be sure I was claiming everything I could claim for and paying the right amount of tax.

It is not essential to have an accountant if you are comfortable filling in your own tax returns and self-assessment forms but I've always preferred to work this way.

What expenses can I claim?

Allowable expenses are anything (within reason) that are necessary for you to write. For example, the following are reasonable expenses:

- PC or laptop
- Office equipment
- Printer cartridges
- Paper
- Postage
- Stationery
- Magazines you need for research purposes
- Books you need for research purposes
- Subscriptions to relevant professional societies
- Writing courses
- Percentage of phone bill used for work
- Percentage of broadband etc used for work
- Travel expenses
- Use of room as office
- Agent fees

NB: This list is by no means exhaustive.

Rules and what expenses are allowable against tax regularly change, so do keep up to date with the current taxation laws. There is a good advice section on tax in *The Writer's Handbook*, which is updated annually.

On the subject of reasonable expenses, I once tried to persuade my accountant that my CD player was an allowable expense – after all, music is my main source of inspiration while I write, but he was not swayed!

What records do I need to keep for the tax man?

You should keep all receipts and also a record of your

earnings. Don't forget you need to make a profit to pay tax. If your outlay exceeds or matches your earnings you won't need to pay tax, although it is still advisable to keep invoices and receipts to prove it.

Some magazine publishers send out end of year earnings to their authors. This same information may be supplied to the Inland Revenue as it's part of their expenses.

Must I pay tax on my competition winnings?

It's very difficult to get a straight answer on this one. Generally, competition winnings are tax free. But if you're claiming your entry fees as an expense and you win – then you should also be declaring your winnings as earnings.

Just to muddy the waters a little more, if you are a professional writer then the tax man won't see any difference between you being paid winnings or earnings. If you are an amateur: i.e. you don't make a profit, then you are probably OK. If you're in any doubt seek guidance from your accountant or the Inland Revenue.

I keep a list of all incomings and outgoings, plus invoices and receipts, which I give to my accountant annually. It's not difficult – it can't be if I can do it! A simple spreadsheet on Excel is fine.

Chapter Twenty-four

How to Deal With Rejection

We all get them – I have hundreds of rejections. And I have come to the conclusion that these days when there are so many good writers submitting to so few slots, that there is a very fine line between a sale and a rejection.

Reasons for rejection

Below are some of the reasons editors have given for rejecting my short stories. I haven't included basic reasons, for example, wrong word length or type, just some of the less obvious ones.

I've classified them into groups for ease.

Predictable
- We could see where your story was going.
- No surprises here.
- Too obvious.

Overused theme
- Familiar theme.
- We see too many of these types of story.
- A well used theme for us.

Undeveloped characters
- We didn't feel we knew enough about Susan to really care about her.
- We felt Susan was unsympathetic.
- We didn't feel Susan would act like this.

Insufficient plot
- We felt your story was slight.
- Not enough to it.
- Too convenient.
- Lightweight.
- Contrived.

Too much plot
- Your story read more like a synopsis.
- Your story lost focus because there was too much going on.

Structure and pace
- Started well, but tailed off.
- Too hectic for our readers.
- Rushed.
- The ending fell flat.

Wrong market
- We don't use ghost stories.
- This was too weird for us.
- We don't take twist-ending stories.
- We only take twist-ending stories.
- We only use female viewpoint stories.

And last, but not least...

Bad Luck
- We've just taken a similar story to this.
- We've recently stopped using this type of story.
- Our new editor doesn't like first person stories.

- Our new editor doesn't like third person stories.
- We've had too many stories about weddings/mothers-in-law/affairs lately.

Actually, I have also come to the conclusion that there is only one reason for rejection – your story isn't right for that editor at that time.

How can I fix these problems?

Here are my solutions to some of the reasons for rejection.

Predictability
This is probably the hardest one to resolve. What is predictable to one editor may not be predictable to another. I often read stories that I think are predictable. The editor obviously didn't. Take a good, long, dispassionate look at your story. Do you think it's predictable? Do your writing friends agree?

If you feel it is not predictable, try another market. If another editor says the same thing, rewrite.

Overused theme
If you're writing for magazines you do need to keep an eye on the market. Try to avoid writing stories with similar themes to ones being published unless you have a completely different angle.

Undeveloped characters
Are you really inside your characters' heads? Or are they being forced into actions they wouldn't make for the sake of the plot?

Sometimes this can mean that you simply haven't put enough of your character on the page. It might help to do a mini biography for each character. For example, Eric is a grumpy old man with a heart of gold who has a passion for golf and growing roses. (He's obviously only grumpy because his wife died!)

Insufficient plot

This is quite tricky. It often means you haven't developed your initial idea into a plot. There is a lot of difference between an idea and a plot that works. It's one that I'm guilty of because I tend to race off on a whim without thinking the story through.

Sometimes you need to combine one idea with another. Having a theme can help. It stops you losing focus. Having a good structure can also help.

Too much plot

This often also means rushed. You've not developed one strand of the plot enough, but have instead thrown in more random elements and it hasn't worked.

Some writers find it impossible to contain themselves to just one storyline and introduce too many. They are often closet novelists!

Structure and pace

This probably means your story is unbalanced. Perhaps you sent it off before it was ready.

Wrong market

You should be researching your market so you should know roughly what the requirements are. Most magazines also issue guidelines for writers and will send you them if you post them a stamped addressed envelope.

Bad luck

Not much you can do about this. It happens to us all. On the plus side it often means that your story was of publication standard, otherwise they'd have given you some other reason for rejection.

So try again with another market.

When to rewrite

If editors offer you the opportunity to rewrite and resubmit your story then grab it with both hands. They won't be saying it just to be polite. They don't have time. They'll only encourage you if they think your work is close to publication standard. Also, you should do it reasonably quickly – this really is a case of strike while the iron's hot. Otherwise an editorial change might lose you the opportunity.

If an editor sends you a rejection, but adds that she'd like to see more of your work, then this generally means they'd like you to send in a new story, rather than rewriting the one she's turned down.

But there is another reason to rewrite. If you have absolute unfailing confidence in a story despite it being continually rejected then go for it until you've exhausted all possible markets. And actually this is impossible, as new markets can appear at any time. My record so far is selling a story that I originally wrote seventeen years previously. The original version and the published version were different, but only because of the updating needed – the basic ideas, premise and characters were the same. It wasn't the best paid, but it was one of the most satisfying sales I've ever had.

Tips on keeping motivated

Don't take rejection personally. If the stories you write aren't suitable for one market, they may well be suitable for another. I am not saying you shouldn't research your market – by the way – just that you might miss it at the first attempt.

Learn from them. If you are lucky enough to get feedback from editors, take heed of their comments and re-write, either for them if they've invited you, or for the next market.

Send out lots and lots of manuscripts. If you have one piece out and it comes back – all hope is lost. If you have two pieces out and one comes back, 50% of hope is lost. If you have 20 or 30 pieces out and one comes back, then – *So what?* The more pieces you have out, the more those individual rejections are diluted. Make sure that you have enough work circulating to generate the, *so what?* factor.

Don't forget that all great authors have rejections.

Competition rejections

Not winning a competition isn't exactly a rejection, but it can still feel as though you've failed. Here are some tips that might help to improve your chances.

Make sure your plot is original.
I have seen comments from several judges of short-story competitions lately, saying that if they read one more hackneyed overused storyline (however wonderfully written) they will scream.

Research your market.
This is hard to do with competition writing, unless you have some inside information about the judge. Don't assume judges will necessarily go for the type of stories they like to write themselves, but do pay heed to any comments they give about what they are looking for.

Conform exactly to the rules
A surprisingly big percentage of manuscripts entered for short-story competition are disqualified because the entrants don't do this. Even if you think you know what

the rules are, go through them again when you put your manuscript into the envelope.

Never send manuscripts out.
This is the only sure fire way to guarantee you won't get a rejection. Naturally, it also guarantees you won't have a success! My point is that whatever we do, we cannot avoid getting rejections. It is the lot of a writer. Ask most successful writers to tell you about theirs and they will probably produce a folder full of rejections, with glee. Rejections are the proof that publishing success in this most challenging of industries doesn't come easy. Let's face it – if it were easy, then getting there wouldn't be anywhere near as satisfying, would it?

Tips from editors

I asked Gaynor Davies, fiction editor of *Woman's Weekly*, and Angela Gilchrist, editor of *The People's Friend*, the following two questions:

1) What is your most common reason for rejecting a story?
2) What makes a good story for your magazine?

Gaynor says:

1) 'The story has no surprises either because it's a well-worn theme or because it is predictable.'

2) The story should have a compelling quality which usually comes from putting a believable character in a situation that is not resolved until the end. Equally important is the style in which the story is written. Writing which has a good flow, which uses just the right amount of imagery (not too much, not too little!) and above all which "shows" rather than "tells" is what we are looking for.

Angela says

1) 'The most common reason for rejecting a story submitted to the "Friend" is because the writer has not taken the time to study the market and has sent us a type of story that we simply never publish. This happens with dozens of stories every week. Even writers who claim to have studied our guidelines make this mistake, and it always results in rejection. The situation is very simple – you may have written the best story in the world, but if it isn't a People's Friend story, we won't buy it.

2) The single most important thing in a good People's Friend story is heart. If it doesn't touch the reader in some way, then it won't be remembered. Strong, likeable characters are essential, too, and so is a happy ending. The aim is always for the reader to feel better for having read a People's Friend story.'

Tips from the experts

Paula Williams says:

'The ability to cope with rejection is one of the most important items in a short-story writer's toolkit. On my desk I have a framed saying which reads *'Many of life's failures are people who did not realise how close to success they were when they gave up.'* And that was me. It seemed that every rejection I received confirmed what I'd always suspected – that I was rubbish.

But then I went on a writers' holiday and met many kind, well published writers who assured me that they too still had to cope with rejection. So now when I get a rejection, do I shrug my shoulders and smile wryly?

Not a bit of it. It still hurts like crazy. But when I've stopped crying (or swearing, depending on my mood) I then have a good hard look at my poor rejected story and if I still believe in it, I send it somewhere else. Again and again and again.

I've recently sold a story to *The Lady* magazine, entitled *Arthur's Last Gamble* that was accepted on its 10th outing. This doesn't mean, of course, that I sent the same story out, unchanged, ten times. That would be insulting to the poor overworked fiction editors. I send a revised version. A story that's targeted at, say, *Take a Break* will probably not work for *The Lady* or vice versa and the version that appeared in *The Lady* was very different from the first submission made two years earlier to *Take a Break*.

So I've learnt two things to enable me to cope with rejection.

1) That revision is a necessary (and, for me, enjoyable) part of the   writing process
2) Never, ever give up.'

David Wass says:

'Many writers have a favourite quote on their wall to encourage them. Mine has been with me since I began. It is by Samuel Beckett and reads simply: "ever fail, try again and fail better." I must have 'failed better', since eventually the 'ever fail' element was overcome. However there will always be rejections, and when one arrives my little quote reminds me not to give up but to "try again".'

Chapter Twenty-five

Excuses Not to Write and What to Do About Them

I haven't got time

Sit down and set a timer for twenty minutes. Start writing and see where it takes you. Everyone has twenty minutes a day. If necessary go to bed twenty minutes later. I promise you this does work.

I can't think of anything to write

This ties in quite well with the above. Do not waste valuable writing time thinking about what to write. Thinking time can be done in the car on the way to work. Traffic jams are particularly good for thinking time. Don't succumb to road rage. Think out plot lines. If you're stuck for characters, simply look around. People under stress make good writing subjects. Traffic jams are perfect writing material.

Some types of housework also provide perfect thinking time, but only the type that you can detach from like ironing or vacuuming.

There are too many distractions

It's probably best to go out. Take your notebook or

laptop to a café or to a park bench. If you can't go out, lock yourself in the bathroom. Or perhaps try working late at night or early in the morning.

I'm too tired

Get used to being tired. It's quite possible to function while being exhausted – as any new parent will tell you. You might not be at your best, but that doesn't really matter with writing. In fact, it can even be an advantage. If you're tired, your mind will tend to wander away from its usual pathways. You can come up with some highly original storylines!

Everything else (in the world) is more interesting than writing

This is one of the worst ones to get over because when you feel like this, then everything else *is* more interesting than writing. Cutting your nails, polishing the keyboard, putting all the paper clips the right way up in your drawer. The only suggestion I can make is that you try the twenty-minute timer trick and hope that you get hooked up in it. Incidentally, this particular problem is most likely to happen when you are about to start a piece of writing so another possible solution is never to start a session by finishing a piece. Always leave it in the middle – then you don't ever have to start anything at the beginning of a session.

By the way, one of my silliest displacement activities involved cleaning my keyboard. I decided to do this properly (I must have been really tired of writing that day) and took the keys off it to immerse in soapy water. Now, I'm a touch typist so I didn't anticipate having a problem putting them back in the right place. However, I didn't realise that I didn't know where things like the semi colon and question mark were – I usually cheat and look at these. So it was more of a problem than I'd anticipated. Also keyboards don't take kindly to being dismantled. My return key wouldn't go back properly and was never the same again.

It's too much like hard work

Writing is the hardest work in the world. But if it wasn't, then it wouldn't also be the most satisfying, most rewarding, most thrilling, most all-absorbing work in the world – need I go on….?

Tips from the experts

Kath Kilburn says:

'Don't let fear of producing something of dubious quality stop you from starting to write. It's very easy to let the idea of that rough first draft – perish the thought that anyone might actually see it! – overwhelm you to the point where you can hardly pick up a pen at all. That would be to miss the point of the first draft. Once you have the bare bones of a story written, it's so much easier then to go back to it and improve, tweak, fine-tune, or even give it a major overhaul. It's what we all do. No one produces brilliant (or even half-decent) fiction without a lot of editing and re-writing.'

Chapter Twenty-six

More Tips From the Experts – on – Well, Just About Everything, Really!

Steve Beresford
On rules to becoming a writer

'I reckon there are two basic rules to becoming a writer.
1) Read
2) Write

If you don't enjoy reading – and by 'enjoy' I mean you read constantly and couldn't live without books and stories to read – then don't start writing. And the best way to learn to write is to actually write.

And don't take up writing because you think: 'I can do better than that.'

Do it because you think: 'I wish I could be as good as that.'

Yes, you might write completely unreadable, unbelievable rubbish to start with – I know I did – but that's how you learn. Characterisation and setting, voice and style, and all the technical things will come with practice and confidence. The more you write the better you'll get at it.

Write, write, write, write. It gets easier. Honest. Although at the same time it also gets harder because your standards get higher accordingly.'

Kath McGurl
On selling my first piece

'When I got my first cheque from a published piece of writing, I was over the moon. I went around with a stupid grin on my face for weeks – even though the cheque wasn't that big, and I earn far more from my day-job. It was just the sheer excitement of knowing that someone valued what I'd written enough to want to pay me for it. What a buzz!

A good friend of mine told me not to simply pay the cheque into my bank account and forget about it. Spend it, she said, on something special you can keep, so that in years to come you can look at what you bought and say, my writing paid for that.

I took her advice, and splashed out on some jewellery. And it's worked. Whenever I wear that piece (a silver necklace with a little diamond embedded) I remember that it was paid for by the proceeds of my first sale.'

Jill Butcher
On the difference between real life and fiction

'In a story you are forcing real life into a shape that has meaning. That's why we like fiction – it has a meaning, or a message. Real life is so unsatisfactory – pleasure can be undeserved, effort unrewarded, evil unpunished and love unrequited. Problems can go on and on for ever, unresolved and unexplained. Real life makes no sense at all! Not so with fiction. In a story problems may not be solved completely, but they are always resolved. The reader must be left with a satisfying emotional response. You can make up the characters

and the plot, but you can't make up the emotion. That
has to be real.'

Lynne Hackles
On how to get ideas

'Harry wouldn't care for an oriental dragon snarling at
him across the landing.' That's what my friend, Janie,
said to me the other day when she was telling me of her
plans to brighten the communal landing in her block of
flats. I'm always seizing bits of dialogue and this one
made a perfect opening line for a short story.

Friends have ceased to be surprised when I pull out
notebook and pen when they're talking. 'What did I
say?' they ask. It could have been anything. A perfect
opening line like Janie's, or a few words which click
and make me think, I can make a story out of that.

If it's another writer I'm talking to when an idea
appears we agree a time-span. 'If you haven't used that
in three month's time, I'm having it.' This often gives
me the added incentive to get on with writing the story.
So, if you'll excuse me, now I have to go and plague
Harry with that dragon.'

Paula Williams
On ideas

'If I live to be 110, I will never run out of ideas for
stories. They come from everywhere, but especially my
friends and family whom I use shamelessly. In fact, my
entire family history is chronicled on the pages of
Woman's Weekly et al. I'm also an intensely nosy
person and, like so many writers, a shameless
eavesdropper.

For instance, I was in my local pub a while back,

when an angry voice rang out across the bar. 'Of course,' the man said, 'Everyone knows Florence Flimflam killed the Farm Shop.' I thought this was such a weird thing to say, and not only because I know Florence (not her real name, of course) who's incapable of killing a spider, least of all a Farm Shop. But the phrase stuck in my mind and developed into a two-part murder mystery story which was published in *Woman's Weekly* in April 2008.

I called the Florence Flimflam character Mildred Hempitt (based on two road names, Mildred Crescent and Hempitt Lane that I noticed one day when stuck in a traffic jam) and came up with a 'cliff-hanger' for the end of chapter one that made me laugh when I wrote it and which I still enjoy now.

In it, my two characters, Will and Kat, are worried about Will's father, who didn't come home the night before. They go into the old Farm Shop to get a leg of lamb out of one of the freezers and find the door unlocked.

"[Will said] 'I didn't think to check in here. That's probably as far as the old fool could stagger last night. What's the betting we find him stretched out in here?'

We did indeed find him stretched out in there. We also found a leg or two. But they didn't belong to a lamb.

Instead, they were sticking out of one of the freezers, clad in thick grey tights and wearing what my mum would call a nice sensible pair of shoes."

And, of course, the body in the freezer turns out to be poor Mildred Hempitt! It was such fun to write, I'm already working on the next one, using the same set of characters – although, not, alas, poor Mildred.'

Linda Lewis, aka Catherine Howard
On ideas

I use a million different ways to come up with story ideas. Often I start with an unusual setting like an auction room or a pet shop, but then again it might be a headline, a time of year, or a title, or a character. As a full time writer, my main problem is that I get too many ideas, and spend far too much time wondering and worrying about which one to tackle next.'

Sue Houghton
On ideas

Become a Nosey Parker. For example, overheard in a supermarket this very morning:
Young man on mobile (bottle of wine and a trifle in shopping basket): 'No, I won't be coming in today, Boss. I'm in such terrible pain I can hardly lift my head off the pillow.'

He saw me eavesdropping, ended the call and winked at me. Why was he lying? Who was the wine for? The boss's wife perhaps?

Julie Dickens
On writing groups

'There is nothing more valuable to a short-story writer than sharing his or her work with like-minded others. My advice would be to join a writing group. It's a great buzz when others find your work entertaining and the feedback, both positive and negative, goes a long way towards making your story saleable.'

Elaine Everest
On Adult Education classes

My Adult Ed classes have been so well attended over

the years that since September 2007 we split them into Beginners, Intermediate and 'Write to get Published.' This class has done so well and all my ladies have now been published at least once in women's magazines.

Their success is down to studying the publication they feel they most identify with and concentrating on submitting to that one publication. Only when they are receiving favourable replies – even if they are nice rejections – can they move to a second magazine.

We often study successful writers, looking at their style and discussing why they are good at their craft.

Ginny Swart
On working with other writers

'The writing group I am lucky enough to belong to is the Wild Geese. We act as critical bouncing boards for each other and aren't afraid to brutally rip and shred stuff put up for comment. Some of the girls are great at proof-reading, spotting duplicate words too close together, or noticing inconsistencies, which are difficult to see for yourself when you get too close to your own story. And basically they say if the ending works or not, or if there isn't enough emotion. And when we get rejections, we commiserate and when we sell something, we all rejoice for each other. Which is really nice because most of us admit our families are not wildly interested in acceptances or rejections. My husband just says, "A sale? Oh that's nice" without lifting his head from the newspaper. We pop the corks on the cyber champagne and pass around the chocolates!

And half the battle of getting an acceptance is to send the right story to the right magazine.'

Linda Mitchelmore
On writing with emotion

'It helps to think of the senses when you have finished your story – sight, touch, hearing, smell, taste – are they all in there somewhere? If not, rectify.'

Georgie Foord
On never wasting an opportunity

'Whatever you write down, in a notebook on the bus, a description on the back of an envelope, an idea that comes to you from nowhere, a name, a title, or a five-minute class workshop, can turn into a sellable story. Transfer all your jottings to your computer, or type up your notes, then when you sit at the computer with your mind a complete blank, you will have something to work on.

Many of my stories start out this way.'

Rachel Lovell
On change

'I have found that lots of my stories concentrate on people in their late forties and fifties and I wonder if this is because this can often be a period of change, when people find themselves, for various reasons, to be moving on. A short story is always about change of some description – things should never be quite the same after the story has unfurled.'

Also from Rachel
On style

'I try to *show* rather than *tell* in my writing. *Showing a scene* rather than *telling a story* breathes life into the characters and builds a world in which both the writer and the reader can lose themselves for a while.'

Kath Kilburn
On writers block

'Got just the germ of an idea but no clue how to follow it up? What I do is take a break from my usual manner of writing. So, if I've been writing longhand recently in my A4 pad (and I love an A4 pad above most things) then I sit at the computer and force the story to go somewhere. I might write the most unlikely stuff but something in there will generally be useable. If, on the other hand, I've done quite a bit of straight-to-the-computer stuff recently, I'll take to the sofa with my A4 pad and a purple pen. Don't know why this works, but those pesky storylines and endings seem to come more easily if I jolt myself out of my writing routine.'

Penny Alexander
On knocking things down

'I'd say there's a need to knock things down before building up again – rather like toddlers with a pile of bricks before they get serious with the Lego! I prefer to start work in any way BUT left-to-right order until clear connections are made. I find this makes the actual writing well, if not easy, at least less likely to take off into devious pathways!'

Geraldine Ryan
On minor characters

'A minor character must provide information not data. 'It's raining again,' is data. 'It's raining again so why is Jane wearing those dark glasses for the second day running?' That's information. Already the reader can smell a story.

Always keep the plot in mind at all times and if your

minor characters aren't doing something to further it, then either get rid of them (see below) or *give* them something to do.

In a murder mystery, for example, this can be to sum up events so far. Or they can be a useful sounding board for your main characters to use as a way of revealing what's going on inside them. Get them to ask the right questions that will tease out the answers you want that will open up your story.

Every story needs conflict. A minor character can be used to set up the conflict. "If that skinny shop assistant with the false nails hadn't sneered when Mary enquired about the price of the lipstick, she'd probably have never even been provoked into looking at her reflection in the mirror once she got home.'

Limit your minor characters. Sometimes you may have to make two characters into one because you simply don't have the words left.

It might break your heart to lose that comical Mrs Baloney with her fondness for butterscotch sweets and her quirky style of dress, but you're just going to have to get over it.

You can't write for the magazine market unless you have a thick skin and don't mind losing your best prose or your favourite minor character.

Don't feel obliged to describe your minor characters in physical detail. Get them *doing* something to capture their essence, rather than have them being static.

Finally, a minor character doesn't necessarily have to be *physically* present in the story. Someone who is no longer in the main character's life, either because of being dead or having moved on, can still exist in the mind of the main character as a powerful catalyst.'

And the last word goes to:

Linda Povey
On 'my golden rules'

'Never put aside a story that's not working. Make it work!

Write the first draft as your greatest fan, the final draft as your harshest critic.

Your opening will get your story read. Your ending will get it sold. Ensure both are gripping!

Make 'em laugh, make 'em cry, surprise them!
Know your market.'

And the very last word, from me, is:

Write from the heart, write what you love and never settle for second best. Then it won't matter whether you sell it or not, because the joy is in the writing itself.

Having said that, if you do these things there's a very good chance you will sell.

Good luck.

Who's Who

Name	Area of expertise
Adrian Magson	novelist, short-story and feature writer. ww.adrianmagson.com
Adam Millward	short-story and feature writer
Angela Gilchrist	editor of *The People's Friend*
Cathryn Cooper	novelist, erotic novelist, short-story writer and editor
Celia Bryce	short-story writer
David Kendrick	short-story writer and novelist
David Wass	short-story writer, erotic short-story writer
Elaine Everest	short-story writer
Elizabeth Dale	short-story writer, children's writer
Francine Lee	short-story and feature writer
Gaynor Davies	fiction editor of *Woman's Weekly*
Georgina Foord	short-story and feature writer
Geraldine Ryan	short-story writer
Ginny Swart	short-story writer
Hilary Halliwell	short-story and feature writer
Ian Burton novelist,	short-story writer, competition judge, creative writing tutor
Jan Wright	short-story writer

Jane Wenham Jones	novelist, short-story writer, columnist for *Writers News* and author of *Wannabe a Writer?*
Janice Day	short-story writer
Jean Dynes	short-story writer and my first tutor
Jean Saunders	novelist, short-story writer, columnist for *Writers News*, competition judge
Jennie Bohnet	short-story writer
Jill Butcher	short-story writer and tutor
Jill Stitson	short-story writer and feature writer
Joyce Begg	short-story writer
Julie Dickens	short-story writer
Kath Kilburn	short-story writer
Kath McGurl	short-story writer
Linda Lewis aka Catherine Howard	short-story and feature writer
Linda Mitchelmore	short-story and feature writer
Linda Povey	short-story writer
Liz Smith	fiction editor of *My Weekly*
Lynne Hackles	short-story and feature writer
Margaret Mounsdon	short-story writer
Marylin Fountain	short-story writer
Mhari Grant	short-story writer, poet and creative writing tutor
Paula Williams	short-story and feature writer
Penny Alexander	short-story writer
Rachel Lovell	short-story writer
Ron Edwards	short-story writer and erotic short-story writer
Rosie Edser	short-story and feature writer

Sandy Neville	short-story writer and competition winner
Steve Beresford	short-story writer
Sue Houghton	short-story writer
Sue Moorcroft	novelist and short-story writer
Teresa Ashby	needs no introduction to anyone who reads short stories!
Tina Wade	short-story writer and my first inspiration

Further Reading/Research

Books

The Writer's Handbook, published by Macmillan
Writers' and Artists' Yearbook, published by A&C Black
Writer's Market UK, published by David and Charles
Wannabe a Writer? Published by Accent Press
Teach Yourself Creative Writing, published by Teach Yourself

Magazines

Writers' Forum
Writers' News
The New Writer
Mslexia
Writing Magazine

Websites

www.bbc.co.uk/writersroom

**More titles in the
Secrets to Success Writing Series
from Accent Press…**

9781907016196

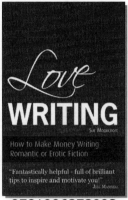

9781906373993

9781906373627

9781906125127

www.accentpress.co.uk

The Writer's ABC Checklist

Lorraine Mace &
Maureen Vincent-Northam

An easy-to-use comprehensive guide for writers on preparing and presenting their work to agents, publishers and print media.

Regardless of the writer's level or ability, there is something extremely daunting about putting together a submission. It doesn't matter if it is for an article for a magazine, or short story for a competition, a humorous anecdote, a play or TV script, a novel or non-fiction book, *The Writer's ABC Checklist* will provide answers to questions you didn't even know you should ask.

With its A–Z format, references can be found quickly and effortlessly. Unfamiliar terms are explained and bullet points at the end of most sections provide a quick reminder of the main items covered.

This unique book is packed with writing tips and is something no aspiring writer can afford to be without.

ISBN 9781907016196 £9.99

Love Writing – How to Make Money Writing Romantic or Erotic Fiction

Sue Moorcroft

Love sells and sex sells and you can earn your living writing about them in novels, novellas and short stories as well as serials for magazines, anthologies and websites.

This book holds the secrets of how to achieve success.

As well as drawing on her experience as a fiction writer and creative writing tutor, in this 'must-have' book Sue has included questions from aspiring writers – with illuminating responses from published writers and industry experts.

Romantic fiction encompasses everything from chart-topping chick lit and romantic comedies, through gritty sagas, sweeping historicals and smouldering erotica to liver-twisting affairs with vampires. Bright, emotional, involving, intelligent storytelling about love and desire is what readers want and will pay for.

Do you want to know how to create emotional punch? (Or even what emotional punch *is?*) How to control dual time lines? Spring your work out of the slush pile? Write a tender love scene that excites passion rather than hilarity? This book reveals all.

ISBN 9781906373993   £9.99

Wannabe a Writer?

Jane Wenham-Jones
Foreword by Katie Fforde

This hilarious, informative guide to getting into print is a must-have for anyone who's ever thought they've got a book in them.

Drawing on her own experiences as a novelist and journalist, **Writing Magazine's** agony aunt **Jane Wenham-Jones** takes you through the minefield of the writing process, giving advice on everything from how to avoid Writers' Bottom to what to wear to your launch party.

Including hot tips from authors, agents and publishers at the sharp end of the industry, **Wannabe a Writer?** tells you everything you ever wanted to know about the book world – and a few things you didn't...

Contributors include writers Frederick Forsyth, Ian Rankin, Jilly Cooper and Jill Mansell and publishers Harper Collins, Hodder Headline and Simon & Schuster as well as leading journalists and agents.

ISBN 9781905170814 price £9.99

www.wannabeawriter.co.uk

Successful Novel Plotting

Jean Saunders

Lost the plot? Get help with this invaluable writers' guide and in no time you'll be turning out real page-turners.

What is it about a good book that hooks the reader and makes them want more? *A good plot.*

Every best-selling author from Agatha Christie to Terry Pratchett knows the importance of a strong story.
But for the budding author it can be daunting and even confusing.

How do you turn that seed of an idea into a great epic?

This authoritative guide will help steer new writers through the minefield of the writing process.

Using examples from her own work, and that of other top authors, Jean explains how to create memorable characters, generate cliff-hangers and keep up a pace that will hook readers.

Jean Saunders is an award-winning author of more than 600 short stories and 100 novels. She's best-known as Rowena Summers, the writer of many novels based in the West Country, and Rachel Moore, author of wartime sagas set in Cornwall. Her WW1 saga Bannister Girls was short-listed for the Romantic Novel of the Year award. Jean now lectures on writing and writes a monthly column for Writing Magazine.

ISBN 978190637627 price £9.99.

How to Write a Pantomime

Lesley Cookman

This book clearly explains how to plan and deliver a successful, traditional pantomime script.

There are thousands of pantomimes staged throughout the world every year, most of them in Britain. Most groups, whether they be amateur drama societies, schools, Women's Institutes or Village Hall committees are constantly on the lookout for something fresh and original. This is often a matter of economics, as professional pantomimes can be costly in terms of performing rights, let alone the cost of scripts. This book is aimed at those people who take part in this increasingly popular hobby, and at the writer who wishes to write a pantomime, either for a local group, or, indeed, for mass publication.

Lesley Cookman has been writing, directing and performing in pantomime for many years. Formerly a freelance journalist, she was for a time editor of *The Call Boy*, the magazine of the British Music Hall Society, and her pantomimes have been performed not only across the British Isles, but in Australia and America. Lesley has written features, short fiction, pantomimes, a musical, a non-fiction book and is currently writing the highly acclaimed Libby Sarjeant murder mystery series for Accent Press.

ISBN 96781906125127 price £9.99

For more information about our books
please visit

www.accentpress.co.uk